CHILD of
the DREAM

A MEMOIR
of 1963

CHILD of the DREAM

A MEMOIR of 1963

SHARON ROBINSON

Scholastic Inc.

Insert photos ©: 1: J. R. Eyerman/Getty Images; 2: Hulton Archive/Getty Images; 3 top: Associated Press/AP Images; 3 bottom: Bettmann/Getty Images; 4 top: Harry Harris/AP Images; 4 bottom: Afro Newspaper/Gado/Getty Images; 5 top: Transcendental Graphics/Getty Images; 5 bottom: Peter Simon; 6 top: Courtesy Sharon Robinson; 6 bottom: Courtesy Sharon Robinson; 7 top: Courtesy Sharon Robinson; 7 bottom: Courtesy Sharon Robinson; 8 top: John Rooney/AP Images; 8 bottom: John Rooney/AP Images; 9: Bettmann/Getty Images; 10 top: Associated Press/AP Images; 10 bottom: Associated Press/AP Images; 11 top: Associated Press/AP Images; 11 bottom: Burton Mcneely/The LIFE Images Collection/Getty Images; 12: Photo Quest/Getty images; 13: Steve Schapiro/Getty Images; 14 top: Courtesy Sharon Robinson; 14 bottom: Courtesy Jackie Robinson Foundation; 15 top: Associated Press/AP Images; 15 bottom: Ted Russell/Getty Images; 16: Courtesy Sharon Robinson.

This book was originally published in hardcover by Scholastic Press in 2019.

ISBN 978-1-338-28281-8

10 9 8 7 6 5 4 3 2 1   20 21 22 23 24

Printed in the U.S.A.   40
This edition first printing 2020
Book design by Maeve Norton

To the children who marched
for freedom in Birmingham,
Alabama, 1963:

Your courage and determination
continue to teach and inspire
us to lift our voices.

CHAPTER 1

Tomorrow is my birthday. I'm turning thirteen. Which makes today—January 12, 1963—the very last day of me not being a teenager.

I stare at myself in the full-length mirror attached to my closet door. I see Dad's smile and Mom's eyes and nose. The gap between my front teeth is distinctly mine. So is being nearsighted. I squint at the rest of my reflection. The way my body has started to curve. The way my skin breaks out around my forehead. There's a look of concern on my face.

Honestly, I'm worried about tomorrow. My older brother, Jackie Jr., started to rebel once he became a teenager. I assume this will happen to me next. Maybe it already has.

I shut the door to my walk-in closet and get dressed for the day in jeans and a T-shirt. *It's best that I thoroughly enjoy these final hours before descending into teenage darkness*, I think to myself. I decide to ride Diamond, my beautiful black-and-white horse with a white diamond shape on his dark black muzzle. He is my four-legged best friend. Together, we push boundaries and release the restlessness that's buried deep inside both of us. Riding Diamond is my definition of freedom.

We're able to have a horse because our home sits on a hill overlooking a lake and is in the middle of six acres of land. My parents, Jack and Rachel Robinson, bought property in Stamford to build this house in 1954, when my father was still playing for the Brooklyn Dodgers. Before that, we lived in an integrated neighborhood in St. Albans, Queens. I was four when we left there—just old enough to have a few memories. But our Connecticut house is where I've spent most of my life. With all of that land, the only thing missing was a horse! We found the perfect spot for the barn and corral. While it was being built, my younger brother, David, and I learned to care for Diamond at a boarding farm a few miles away.

I dress for warmth and adventure, in beat-up riding jeans and two layers of shirts and sweaters. I leave my room, passing by my brothers' rooms as I head down the hallway to the kitchen. Mom is standing at the stove, frying bacon. Usually, Dad would be standing beside her, stirring grits. But he's still in the hospital recovering from knee surgery. Instead, my grandmother shifts between the grits on the stove and fresh biscuits in the oven. Seeing them makes me anxious for an update on Dad. I can't hide my disappointment. I was expecting him home for my birthday.

"Morning," I say.

"Good morning, Sharon." Mom's smile is bright. "You're just in time for breakfast. Please set the table and call your brothers."

After putting five placemats, silverware, and paper napkins on the table, I skip back down the hall, tapping on my brothers' doors and calling out to them. "Jackie! David! Breakfast." Then I turn around and walk back to the kitchen, slipping into a chair at the table.

While I wait for the others, I plan my morning ride. Cascade Road is a winding country road with minimal traffic, no streetlights or sidewalks. It curves up and down hills for a few miles and ends at a bridge over a waterfall—the perfect place for a morning ride.

First I'll head up Cascade to the dirt road, where I can run Diamond and warm him up for a longer ride. I picture it in my head. *Then I'll go check out the road along the reservoir. I want to feel the breeze on my face and Diamond's strong body carrying me as we race down the straightaway.*

My thoughts are interrupted when David bounds into the kitchen and slides into the seat next to me. He is followed by a sleepy Jackie. At ten and sixteen, my brothers are polar opposites. David's ability to make us laugh and his high energy are in sharp contrast to a sullen Jackie, who is a constant worry. I look up and smile at Jackie as he takes a seat across from me. We speak with nods.

Besides Dad, there is another member of the family missing from breakfast. Willette Bailey lives with us during the week, helping Mom with everything from cooking to watching over us. On the weekends, Willette goes home to a section of New York City called Harlem. Sometimes, we trail along with her. Willette's been with us so long, she's like a second mother to me. I know she hates missing my birthday party.

"I've got hockey practice at nine," David announces as Mom places a platter of scrambled eggs and bacon next to a bowl of grits on the table. We pass the plate around, taking large portions of both.

"Am I driving you over to Michael's house?" Mom asks David.

"No, his dad is picking me up."

"I'll take care of Diamond," I offer, scooping hot grits onto my plate.

"He tossed me into the pond yesterday," David reports.

That's the grumpy Diamond. I hope his mood has changed.

"David, that's the third time he's done that. Why don't you bring a bucket of water with you to the stables instead of taking Diamond down to the lake to drink?" Mom suggests.

"Aww, Mom. That's no fun."

"Do as I say, please," Mom replies, then turns to me. "It's below freezing. The dirt roads will be icy," Mom warns. "Use the saddle."

I nod, careful not to make a promise. I prefer to ride Diamond bareback, but I can give the saddle a try today.

"You won't catch me on that crazy horse," Jackie says without lifting his eyes from the food on his plate.

"He is not crazy," I snap.

"Then you are, for riding him without a saddle," Jackie says.

"You're the crazy one for hanging out in those pool halls late at night," I shoot back.

Mom warns us with a stern look.

"Sorry," I say to my brother. I fork grits into my mouth, savoring the buttery taste and grainy texture.

"It's okay, sis," Jackie replies. "How about a game of pool after dinner?"

"You and me?" I ask, surprised. Jackie has little tolerance for bad pool players and, believe me, I am one of those.

"Why not? It's your birthday, right?"

"Cool," I say, touched by this gesture and a bit suspicious. *Why's he being so nice to me?*

"Jackie, I want you to come to the hospital with us tomorrow so we can celebrate Sharon's birthday as a family. Okay?" Mom asks, though it's not really a question. Jackie hasn't been to visit Dad since he went into the hospital two weeks ago.

Jackie says nothing at first. He just stands up and glances briefly at our mother.

I am holding my breath. It's not a conscious thing. It just happens while I anxiously await Jackie's reply. *Please, Jackie. Please,* I pray.

My brother shakes his head. "Can't," he says, walking away from the table. "I have plans."

Air escapes from my lips and I feel deflated like a balloon. I watch Jackie leave, then I turn to face Mom. *There it is,* I think. The look of disappointment on her face. I can't stand it.

"What are you doing today?" I ask my mother, moving the conversation away from Jackie's rejection.

"I have to go on a few errands and visit your dad," Mom says as she tries to recover.

Grandma glances at Mom and they exchange an adult worried look. "How is he?" she asks.

"His knee is infected."

"What!" This is the first time I'm hearing of this complication. I start to panic. My heart races, but I stay glued to my seat.

My dad means the world to me. For years, he was considered one of the best athletes on the planet. Tens of thousands of baseball fans would come from all over to cheer for him playing second base for the Brooklyn Dodgers. How could someone who was once so healthy be stuck in the hospital like this? It doesn't make sense to me.

"It happens sometimes," Mom says. "Your father will have to stay in the hospital until it clears up."

"How long will that take?" David asks.

We all have places to go, but no one moves. I grab hold of the table leg.

"At least another week. Maybe two," Mom replies.

I tear up thinking of my dad in some scary hospital room instead of home with us. David must have seen it, too, because he jumps in with one of his funnies.

"I'll bring him my sword."

I don't even know what that means, but we all laugh at the image of a little boy arriving at his father's hospital bedside ready to save the day. "Why'd you say that?" I ask my brother when everyone stops chuckling.

"So he can protect himself from the doctors," David replies, like it's perfectly logical.

"David, what are you talking about? The doctors are helping your father get well," Mom reminds him.

"Dad was feeling good when he went to the hospital and now he's sick. They must be doing something wrong," David says, slamming his knife down on the table. He stands up, drops his plate into the sink, and leaves the kitchen without saying another word.

"Your father will feel much better when he sees you tomorrow," Grandma tells me.

"We can save the birthday-cake part until we're with Dad," I offer, ignoring the fact that he's not supposed to eat sugar because of his diabetes. *Would a single slice of cake send his blood sugar soaring?*

"Great idea, Sharon," Grandma agrees. "I'm counting on you to help me make this cake."

"Soon as I get back from riding Diamond," I assure her while I gather up my plate and empty glass.

"Don't forget to clean Diamond's stall," Mom adds.

"I won't," I say, and drop my plate in the sink.

"Rachel, you go on. I'll get the dishes," Grandma offers when Mom heads to the sink.

"Thank you. Dinner's six sharp," Mom calls to whoever is within earshot.

"What are we having?" I ask halfway out the door.

"Steak, baked potato, and salad. Does that meet with your approval?"

"Oh yeah," I reply. "It's Candy's favorite, too." If Diamond is my best animal friend, then Candy Allen is my best human friend. She lives a few miles from us and is the only other Black girl in my school. Candy is sleeping over tonight so that when I wake up tomorrow on my birthday, she'll already be here. "When it comes to steak, Candy thinks you have special powers," I say before rushing off to get ready for the barn.

CHAPTER 2

I put on my coat and boots, then stroll down the hill to the stables. I love my Diamond days, but my fingers are freezing before I reach him. I wrap the wool scarf around my face and shove my hands into my jacket pockets. Only my eyes peek over the scarf and they water in protest.

"Morning, Diamond," I say, softly stroking his forehead with my fingers.

He snorts and shakes his head.

"It's cold, but we're going to have some fun anyway."

Diamond's ears shoot forward.

I clean his stall and replenish the food in his trough, then prepare him for our ride.

"This is my birthday weekend, so put on your best behavior. Okay?"

Diamond nudges me with his nose.

"I'm trying to be quick."

I stare into Diamond's eyes, daring him to be the first to blink. I give up and giggle. "I'm not having a party. Dad's in the hospital. Nobody's in the mood for a bunch of girls running around the house. At least Candy's spending the night. We'll make milkshakes and listen to music. Oh yeah, Jackie said we can even play pool. I'm looking forward to it. Even though I'm really worried about Dad."

It helps me, talking to Diamond. I think of him as my horse even though, technically, Diamond was given to my younger brother, David. Diamond came to live with us after our parents attended a dinner party in Greenwich, Connecticut—not far from our house in Stamford. The hostess told my mother about her son, who was now off at college, and how they were keeping his childhood horse out in pasture. The story of this boy and his horse made Mom think of her youngest son, and before the night was over they worked out Diamond joining our family.

I suppose Mom mentioned that I'd been researching horses for years and had volunteered at a petting farm near our house for several summers. But who knows? These mothers were talking about their boys. And truthfully, I don't care how Diamond came to live with us at 103 Cascade Road. Just that he is ours now.

We quickly figured out that this horse was a bit feisty. That trait, which most likely comes from Diamond's years alone and ignored in the pasture, endeared him to us even more. So we've spent the last six months trying to make Diamond feel loved. Some days, he actually returns our devotion. I'm hoping today is going to be one of those good days when the only thing I'll be feeling is the heart-pounding joy of the ride.

I lift Diamond's hoofs and clean out the dirt with a brush and metal pick. When I'm done, I put the brushes away and reward him with a carrot. "Ready to ride?"

I slide the bit into Diamond's mouth past his teeth, then lace the leather straps in front of and behind his ears. I check the saddle. It's frozen. No way am I sitting on that. It will feel like a block of ice on my backside! I look around the stall for something to warm up the saddle, but there's nothing around. "Bareback, it is," I say to Diamond. "Shhh, don't tell Mom." I lead him into the open air and vault onto his back. My right leg swings over his side. As I take up the reins, we set off on an adventure.

With minimal urging, Diamond shifts from a slow gait to a trot. My body rises and falls with his two-step. We head up the hill, then turn onto the dirt road. I scan the road for icy patches. Seeing none, I ease up on the reins and let Diamond rip. In seconds, we're in full gallop, flying like a kite that's caught the breeze. The cold wind whips across my face, but I can barely feel it. I'm too happy. This is the way it's supposed to be.

After pounding the road, steam pours out of Diamond's nostrils. "Ready for the long stretch?" I ask, though it's not an actual question. Diamond doesn't really have a choice as I steer him up Cascade Road, past the North Stamford Congregational Church, where we go to Sunday school and church services, then down toward the road that runs along the reservoir. I've heard that, at night, the road is pitch-black and turns into a lovers' lane. Kids from high school park and kiss in the dark. I can't even imagine the idea of being alone with a boy who isn't one of my brothers. Then I think about the crush I had on my brother's best friend, Bradley Gordon. But Bradley lives in New York City and only thinks of me as Jackie's baby sister.

In the morning, this road remains deserted, so I can race Diamond with little fear of traffic. I make a clicking sound with my tongue and Diamond takes off again. It feels like he lifts all four legs off the ground at the same time. It's a smooth, fast ride. I'm having a great time until Diamond stops abruptly. *Did something scare him?* Without hesitation, he whips around and takes off toward home. I am no longer in charge of the ride. In fact, I can barely hold on. "Oh, please. Oh, please. No. No. No." I squeeze tight against his belly, praying I don't end up on the ground.

In minutes, we reach the part of Cascade Road where mail-boxes and driveways line the street. As we pass the first mail-box, my right leg scrapes against the metal, which tears my jeans and leaves a four-inch gash on the outside of my shin. I cry out in agony. Tears flow. I look down at my ripped riding jeans and see dots of red—blood—seeping through the denim. Diamond presses on, oblivious to my fear and pain. I scream, "Watch out!" but it's too late. A low-lying tree branch zaps me. I fly off Diamond's back and land hard against frozen ground just outside our property line. Luckily, I'm not hurt. I stand up and wipe the dirt from my jeans and the tears from my eyes. *Today is not going as planned*, I think as I limp home.

"What were you thinking?" I shout at myself. "Mom told you not to do that!" *But would it have made a difference if I'd saddled him?* I think. *Who knows?* One thing is for sure: I cannot tell my mother about the long gash on my leg or the blow to my self-confidence.

When I reach the corral, Diamond looks away from me. He is standing just outside the gate. I can't scold him because it's my fault, too. I lead him inside for grooming and look deep into his eyes. "Diamond," I say, releasing a long slow sigh. "We have a lot of work to do."

CHAPTER 3

Cleaned up and bandaged, I join my grandmother in the kitchen so we can get going on my birthday cake. The mixer is on the countertop along with cake flour, butter, milk, and vanilla flavoring. The three women in our house are all great cooks. Mom is good all around, but Willette and Grandma are the bakers. Grandma and I have been cooking together for three years. I know her routines and expectations. She knows my moods. Grandma takes one look at me and knows something's up.

"Did you have a good ride?" she asks as I cozy up next to her.

"Not really," I reply, avoiding eye contact and focusing instead on the open cookbook. I reach into the spice cabinet and pull out the other dry ingredients: salt, baking powder, and sugar.

"Remember the day Diamond arrived?" Grandma says with a chuckle as she hands me the sifter and measuring cup. "You and David were so excited. You took turns hopping on his back."

"He reared straight up in the air as soon as we were settled in the saddle," I say, then laugh along with Grandma. Looking back, it was kind of funny. I pour two cups of cake flour into the measuring cup and slide it toward my grandmother for her approval.

"That horse has a mind of his own. Good thing you watch all those TV Westerns . . . you and David looked like Annie Oakley and the Lone Ranger up there on that horse!" She nods and pushes the measuring cup back to me. Mostly, Grandma trusts me—except when it comes to baking, with its need for perfection.

"He's tough to handle sometimes," I admit, dumping the flour into the sifter.

"Give him time, darling. Horses are like people. It takes time to trust someone else. You and Diamond are just getting to know each other."

"It's been six months," I protest.

"That's a short time. I'm no expert at horse training, but your grandfather was. He worked on a ranch for years before we got married. He used to talk about handling horses. They're strong animals. They can sense when you're afraid or not in control."

"Please don't tell Mom, but I fell off him this morning," I beg. "Cut my leg pretty bad."

"Let me see it."

"It's okay now. I cleaned it up and put on a bandage."

"It could have been much worse," Grandma says. "Not the birthday present you were hoping for. I won't ask if you used the saddle."

"I'm not even sure if it would've helped."

"You've got the makings of a really good rider. Now you need to learn how to communicate better with your horse. But . . . enough about Diamond. We've got to focus on getting this cake made before your mother gets home. She'll want to get in this kitchen to make your birthday dinner."

I love my grandmother and am thankful every day that she came from Los Angeles to live with us. I was ten when Mom went back to graduate school at New York University and decided to bring her mother, Zellee, closer. Willette had been our live-in help, but with Grandma around, we had an extra layer of love and support. The fact that she is an amazing cook is an added bonus!

In her younger days in Los Angeles, Grandma was a highly respected caterer. She worked a number of Hollywood parties. My mother worked with her and had some funny stories to tell about it. Grandma had learned the art of cooking and the restaurant business from her parents. Her dad was a chef on the railroad for many years before the president of Mexico enticed him to open a restaurant in the border town of Nogales. Mom and her brother would help out during their summer breaks. Nana, my great-grandmother, kept a shotgun below the cash register. One summer, she chased a robber out of the restaurant and up the hill until he disappeared.

Birthday cakes are one of Grandma's specialties. My brothers prefer yellow cake with chocolate icing. I prefer a white cake with buttercream icing. Since Dad's diabetes diagnosis, we limit our sugar intake. Grandma does her part and mostly bakes monkey bread, biscuits, apple pie, and pound cake without icing. But she still always makes her famous cakes for our birthdays.

I carefully measure out baking powder, salt, and sugar while Grandma provides a second pair of eyes. Then Grandma blends my dry mix in with her wet ingredients, fluffing it into a creamy batter. Grandma spoons the batter into the greased cake pans and slides them into the oven. I take the bowl of remaining batter with me to the kitchen table.

While I snack on the leftover batter, Grandma pulls out her decorating tools. She will fill her pastry bag with icing and use the attached tools to decorate my cake with pink-and-yellow flowers and green leaves.

"Grandma, is turning thirteen really a big deal?" I ask. I'm still somewhere between "girly girl" and "tomboy." A year ago, Willette and I packed up the last of my dolls. But I also stopped playing touch football with the neighborhood boys. I'm beginning to wonder what's next.

"Sure is, my sweet girl. You're a teenager now. Your body and mind will change as the hormones kick in."

"Grandma, I know all this stuff," I groan.

I'd started my period and needed a bra last year. That was embarrassing enough, but I was mortified when I developed so quickly. That's the real reason why I stopped playing touch football with the boys.

"I know you do, but that was just the beginning. More's coming."

"Like what?" I ask as I lick the last of the batter off the rounded end of the spoon. The bowl is scraped clean.

Grandma joins me at the kitchen table. "Once I got interested in boys, you couldn't tell me anything."

"Honestly, Grandma, I go to school with a bunch of White boys. They're okay to play volleyball with. But I don't know about more than that," I tell her.

She chuckles. "In a way, that's good," Grandma says as she gets up from her chair and walks back to the sink. "But that will change," she adds. "You'll start going to Jack and Jill parties. You'll meet plenty of Black boys. You'll feel more included."

"I just hope I'm not as unhappy as Jackie," I say, getting up to help Grandma wash the dishes. I hand her the mixing bowl I had been eating out of at the table.

"Your brother is a special case. It's tough being named after someone famous. Folks expect so much out of you," she says, looking directly at me.

My brother's full name is Jack Roosevelt Robinson, Jr. He's named after our dad. Jackie Jr. was born shortly before Dad broke the color barrier in Major League Baseball. He's just a little more than three years older than me. By the time I was born, Dad was in his fourth season. Our younger brother, David Raymond Robinson, was born two years after me. David and I were too young to appreciate our father's accomplishments on the field, but we knew he was the first African American player in Major League Baseball. Rookie of the Year in 1947. League MVP in 1949. In 1955, Dad stole home in game one of the World Series and helped the team win their only championship! They even made a movie about him. It was called *The Jackie Robinson Story*. Dad played himself, and Ruby Dee, a famous actress, portrayed Mom. Jackie Jr. was also portrayed in the film. That's how recognizable his name is. That's how much of a spotlight it put on Jackie Jr.

"Yeah, I remember when Jackie Jr. used to play baseball and people would compare him to Dad. That wasn't fair . . . was it?"

"Not at all, but sometimes adults can be insensitive, too. You'll face some of that, too, you know."

"But I'm a girl. No one will expect me to play baseball."

"True, but you're still going to be held to very high standards. I have faith in you," she says, handing me the wet wooden spoons so I can dry them.

"I promise you, Grandma, I will keep working hard," I say, placing the dry spoons in the drawer.

Grandma smiles as I head for Dad's transistor radio. I flick it on and turn the dial away from 1010 WINS news to a station playing pop music. The Chiffons hit the first beats to "It's My Party." The song makes me sad. It's about a girl who gets her heart broken at her own party. I wipe tears off my cheek, feeling selfish. But honestly, I should be having a party tonight for my special birthday and my dad should be here for it.

"Dad was only supposed to be in the hospital for two to three days. It's been over a week. He must be sicker than Mom's letting on."

Grandma looks over at me. "My. My. They do play some sad music on this radio station," she says. "Look, Sharon, you're old enough now that I can be honest about this. Your father's diabetes has complicated the recovery."

"I thought that those insulin shots controlled diabetes."

"They help, but type 1 diabetes is tricky. It's making your father's recovery from this infection harder. He's a strong, determined man. Don't you worry. Your father is not going to lay up in some hospital much longer. He's anxious to get home and back to work."

"I bet he's worried about Jackie." For two weeks, my brother has been "too busy" to visit Dad in the hospital. But too busy with what? All he does is stay out late at the poolrooms and then sleep all day. I suspect that he's failing at school again and might not even be going to class at all.

Grandma nods. She's boiling water for tea and not looking at me. "We all are," she finally admits. "How about we make a deal."

"What's that?"

"Let's celebrate your special birthday and put our worries aside. And when you see your father tomorrow, focus on how happy you are to see him and don't mention your worries about Jackie."

"Deal," I say as "Tell Him" by The Exciters comes on the radio. It's a song about telling a boy that you like him. I slither down in my chair before Grandma can see the look on my face.

CHAPTER 4

Fifteen balls line the inside of the wooden rack. Seven are striped and eight are solid, counting the black eight ball in the middle. Jackie Jr. carefully removes the mold and places the white cue ball on its spot. He stands back and studies the setup before signaling to me.

"You break," Jackie says while rubbing a square block of chalk on the tip of his cue stick.

For me, playing pool is an occasional thing. It is a way of life for Jackie. A lifestyle that fits his rebelliousness. A way to gamble and make money. He plays at home and in pool halls. Jackie is good. He usually takes charge of the game, including the break. So why is he changing things up now?

"Come on, sis. It's your birthday. I'll go easy on you."

"Sure, but Candy and I want to play a game of pool by ourselves." I glance over at my best friend. She arrived at my house for my birthday sleepover right after Grandma and I cleaned up from baking. She is perched on top of a tall barstool. Her long legs almost reach the ground. She flashes me an encouraging smile.

I grab the chalk and put some on my stick. I know using the chalk makes you less likely to scratch and I need all the help I can get!

"First game is you and me. I want to see if you remember all I taught you."

Now I'm really intimidated. I run my fingers along the edge of the green felt and slowly move down the length of the table.

My big brother is so handsome and strong. He used to like playing baseball and football, but lately only pool interests him. In pool, he's not trying to compete with Dad or live up to his name. But spending time in the pool halls puts Jackie in a sketchy adult world of dark rooms full of smoke and alcohol. He and Dad argue about this lifestyle and his disregard for the rules. In three years, Jackie had been in and out of two high schools, including a recent suspension from boarding school. He is back home and going to Rippowam High School, but not doing much better. We're all afraid he'll drop out of school altogether when he turns seventeen. Then, what—the army? I hate the tension. There are nights when I wait up for Jackie to get home safely, then cover my head so I won't hear the argument.

"Aim here," Jackie says. He points to the red dot in the middle of the white ball. "And be careful with the felt."

We are on the lower level of our two-story house, in our playroom. It's right next door to my dad's trophy room. But most of the space in here is taken up by massive adult toys like Jackie's pool table and Dad's indoor golfing range. I claim the soda fountain as my spot. I'm the self-proclaimed Queen of Milkshakes.

When our house was being built, they found huge boulders above- and underground throughout the property. The contractors smashed up some of them and used them as building material. But a few of the boulders were too big. Like the one that juts into the playroom. The contractors couldn't move it, so they built the interior wall around it. There are two more that stick out on our front lawn. During summer baseball games, we designate one of the boulders as home plate and one as first base. You don't dare slide into either one. Instead, we touch base with our hands.

I look up and see David leaning against the massive rock. He gives me the thumbs-up for luck.

I lean over the table, and my right hand helps balance the cue stick on my hip. The long stick threads along my body and lands between the fingers of my left hand. I test its movement. I have no illusion of winning this game, but a clean break would be nice.

"Looking good, Shar," Jackie says. He steps back and crosses his arms over his chest.

I stay focused. The stick is in the circular space created by my thumb and index finger. The remaining fingers lift into a bridge. I pull the stick back slowly, and then shove it forward. *Wham!* The white ball busts open the triangle of colored balls, sending them flying in all directions. My heart pounds. I hold my breath as the solid yellow ball rolls toward the middle pocket. It teeters on the edge, then drops in. I jump up and down.

"Great shot!" Candy yells.

David hustles over and slaps me on my back.

Even Jackie's face is plastered with a grin. "What's your next shot?" he asks.

I study the position of the pool balls. The orange one is near the far right pocket, but it's not a sure shot. "I'm not calling," I say as I bend back down to take a second shot. That means I don't have to pick which pocket the ball goes in. Jackie is so good at pool, he always calls his shots before he shoots. This time the balls clack into one another, shifting positions, but none go in. I step away from the table as Jackie steps up to it.

"Number fifteen, left corner pocket," he says. He lands the ball. "Ten, right corner."

With little effort, Jackie knocks his seven striped balls into the pockets one by one until he's down to just the eight ball.

"Eight in the middle," he calls out, and the magic happens again.

"Wow!" I say, wishing schoolwork came as easy for Jackie. Maybe then he wouldn't hate it so much.

"Don't sweat it, sis. This is what I do."

"You're the best," I say.

"Candy, do you want to give it a shot?"

She laughs. "No, thank you."

"What about you, Dave?"

"Sure." At ten years old, he has no fear.

I watch my brothers play, Jackie confidently picking his shots and David trying his best to keep up. *I wish it could be like this all the time*, I think to myself. While the boys play, Candy and I scoop vanilla ice cream into the blender. I add milk and vanilla flavoring, cover the blender, and switch it on. Game-used baseball bats from Dad's playing days fan out on the wall behind us. I don't usually spend much time looking at the stuff on the walls down here, but whenever we have company over, it's one of the first things everyone wants to see. Candy is over so much, she barely even notices it anymore.

Before I know it, Jackie has beaten his little brother. It was even faster than our game!

"Got to split," Jackie tells us after drinking his milkshake. "Have fun, but don't mess with my table."

I watch my brother climb the stairs. He stops on the top step and turns away from Dad's trophies.

"Thanks for playing pool with me, Jackie," I say to him.

He smiles. "Someday, I'll have just as many trophies for playing pool as Dad's got for his ten years in big-league baseball."

I stare at his back, wondering if they really give out trophies for winning games of pool in Stamford, Connecticut.

"Come on, Sharon. Let's get your birthday party started!" Candy shouts. She's a good friend.

CHAPTER 5

Candy and I race upstairs to my room. I sit down on the edge of my bed and watch her rummage through her suitcase on the floor.

"Ah," she says as she pulls out a square package wrapped in blue paper with a red bow. "I brought you a present."

"Gee, that was nice. This isn't really a party, you know," I say.

"I was wondering about that," Candy says. "You usually have a sleepover with a bunch of girls. How come you only invited me this year?"

"With Dad so sick, I didn't feel like having a party," I tell her.

"I'm kind of happy you didn't have another sleepover. Is that selfish?" Candy's voice lowers. "You remember what happened at your party last year."

"Oh, I remember," I say, dropping to the floor to sit by my friend. Last year, Candy's mom had been very sick and died unexpectedly. I touch her shoulder with my hand. "That was the saddest birthday party. We didn't know what to say to you. It was so hard to believe what was happening. You were so brave."

"Not really," Candy says. "I just didn't know what else to do. Then when I got home, I had to pretend to be brave because I'm the oldest. I didn't want to upset Kimberly. She was only five when Mom died. I didn't have a thirteenth birthday party either."

"I forgot about that," I say.

"Well, my birthday was only three months after Mom died. I just wasn't interested in a party."

"I understand." I lean over to give her a hug. "I'm so happy we're friends."

"Me, too." Candy's expression changes to one of concern. "How's your dad? When's he coming home?" Candy asks.

"Who knows?" I reply. I wish he was home now. "He's got some kind of infection that's linked to diabetes. It's a complication." I pick up my hairbrush.

"That's not good," Candy says as she gets up and heads to the bathroom. "My mom died from some kind of infection."

My heart skips a beat. My brush drops to the floor. I slowly bend down to pick it up. "Great . . . now I feel worse," I say, and sit on my bed.

"I didn't mean to scare you. I'm sure he'll be okay. I'll be right out." Candy closes the bathroom door.

When Candy comes out, I'm still sitting on my bed with the hairbrush in my hands. "I didn't know you could die from an infection," I mumble.

Candy sits next to me. "It was a stupid thing to bring up. Your dad is on antibiotics at the hospital. That's different. My mom was at home when she was sick."

"I'm not so confident. Mom's been quiet about Dad's condition. I think she's very worried and hiding something from us." I don't like talking about this, but it's better than holding it inside.

"I doubt it," Candy says as she takes her socks off.

"What's it like?" I ask her.

"Huh?"

"Not having your mom in your life?"

"It's hard." Candy sighs. "We don't really talk about it at my house. Dad works a lot. Eddie spends too much time alone in his room. Kim doesn't remember Mom as much as me. Aunt Billie helps out as much as she can, but sometimes, I find myself crying for no reason."

"You must miss her," I say, looking up.

"Every day," Candy says. "I'm so lucky to have you and your family."

I laugh. "You were going to be my friend no matter what. Remember how my mother spotted you playing in your front yard on her way home from shopping at Bloomingdale's?"

Candy had just moved to town and my mom was on high alert for a Black friend for me.

"Yeah, that story," Candy says, and we both fall over with laughter.

"I think it was your long wavy hair that got Mom's attention. She told me that you had braids down to your waist. Mom called Mrs. Dickerson, who gave her the whole scoop, including your street address."

"What else did she say?"

"That you had a younger sister and brother and your dad was the only Black dentist in town," I begin. "She also told Mom that your mother was a social worker and that you'd recently moved up here from Richmond, Virginia."

"Mrs. Dickerson's amazing. I bet she knows every Black family in Stamford," Candy says. "And then after all that, we ended up in the same class at school!"

"I can't believe that was three years ago already. It felt so great to finally have another Black girl in my school. And it was even better that we had already met."

"It felt good to me, too," Candy says. "So, almost-birthday girl, how do you feel about turning thirteen?"

"Excited. Worried. Confused."

"I understand." Candy nods in agreement. "I was worried that a lot more would be expected of me. I was already baby-sitting Kimberly and Eddie after school." Candy pauses and a big grin spreads across her face. "Hey, look," she says, holding up her gift. "I brought you music! If we're going to start going to parties, we need to learn how to dance!"

"Thanks," I say as I tear the wrapping off the package, already knowing it's a stack of 45 records—I can tell by the size of them. I quickly flip through to see what songs Candy brought me.

"If I Had a Hammer" by Peter, Paul and Mary gets an appreciative nod, but when I spot the Motown hits "Soldier Boy" and "Baby It's You" by the Shirelles, "You've Really Got a Hold on Me" by the Miracles, and "Stubborn Kind of Fellow" by Marvin Gaye, I want to dance. We live for these small round plastic records. Motown singers are our way into the Black world.

I pull my record player from the closet and put the needle on "Baby It's You," then we start singing along and moving our bodies to the beat.

Our arms swing over our heads and back down to our sides.

"You know Dolan's having another school dance this year,"

I shout over the music. Dolan Junior High is the school Candy and I have been attending for two years now.

"Ugh," Candy replies. "The last one was awful. Standing in a corner with our backs plastered to the wall. It was so embarrassing that no one asked us to dance."

"I'm not going to it," I say as the record ends. Candy continues to move about my bedroom while I squat down to change the song.

"You have to go," Candy says.

"They can't make me," I protest.

"I'm dreading it, too, but every eighth-grade student is required to attend," she tells me.

"I hate that they would make a stupid dance mandatory," I shout, slapping the next 45 onto my record player. "I'm going to Mr. Moon to tell him that I think it's unfair to force us to attend."

"Good luck," Candy says.

"You should still go, though. The boys may ask you to dance this time. Your skin color is closer to white than mine," I say.

"I'm still a Negro," she reminds me.

"True," I say as Marvin Gaye's soothing voice calls out, "Say yeah yeah yeah!"

"Yeah yeah yeah . . ." we call back to him.

Before we know it, we're laughing and swinging our narrow hips as if we don't have a thing to worry about.

CHAPTER 6

I wake realizing its Sunday, January 13. Today is my actual birthday! That's what I should be excited about. But instead, I think about my dad.

He is my rock. I can hear his voice in my head saying, "Just put your finger in my iced tea and I won't need any sugar." He says that to me all the time. I wish he was home to make birthday pancakes with me. I feel miserable all over again.

I get out of bed and grab my bathrobe to help protect me from the chilly morning air. Mom turns the heat down at night. Dad's usually the first up in the mornings, so he turns the temperature back to seventy, our rambling house always taking its time to heat up. The coolness is another reminder of Dad's absence. After going to the bathroom, I stop next to the bed and shake Candy.

"Time to get up," I tell her. "Your dad will be here soon."

She yawns and stretches, then peers up at me with sleepy eyes. "What time is it?"

"It's eight. We should get dressed and have breakfast before your dad comes."

"Oh yeah, happy birthday."

"Thanks."

Candy sits up in bed. "Are you going to Sunday school?"

"Yep," I say, and disappear into the bathroom. When I come back out, Candy is up, making her bed.

"Want to come to church with us?" Candy asks.

"Believe me, it's tempting. Your church is way cooler than ours, but I'm meeting Christy so we can walk to our church together. And then afterward, Mom's driving us to Mount Vernon to visit Dad in the hospital."

Thirty minutes later, I wave goodbye to Candy and head to the end of the driveway to watch for Christy. She lives about six houses up the street, but the houses are pretty far apart. It's about an eight-minute walk. Christy and I have been best friends since we were five, but lately we haven't been as close. When she arrives, we hug and continue the five-minute walk up the hill to church.

At Sunday school, I can barely concentrate on anything the teacher says. All I can think about is seeing Dad. *How will he look? Will he be okay?* The morning is a fog.

Afterward, we're off to Mount Vernon in New York to see

Dad. Mom's driving Dad's Cadillac. Grandma sits beside her. They're talking about Grandma's plans to visit her friends in Brooklyn next week. David and I chat in the back seat.

"I'm mad at Jackie," I say softly to my little brother.

"He didn't come home last night," David whispers.

"Where is he?" I ask.

David shrugs.

I don't know how to interpret Jackie's behavior, but it's so frustrating. I don't know if Jackie is angry, sad, or just plain mean. Can't he just be normal? Maybe I do expect too much from him.

"We hear you," Mom calls from the front seat. Grandma is looking over at Mom, probably also wondering where Jackie is.

Mom glances back at Grandma. "He called this morning to apologize. Said he stayed over at a friend's house. I'll deal with him later," Mom says.

I see Grandma lift her eyebrows.

"You're not mad at him?" I ask incredulously.

"Worried. Disappointed," Mom replies.

"I guess that's not the same as mad," I say after thinking about her reply.

"It is different," she tells me. "But it's important that we don't let his problems take away from your birthday celebration. Or add to your father's distress. Okay?"

"Okay," I say, still shocked at Mom's honesty. It's the first time she's shared her feelings with me. I lean my head against the window, not sure what to do with this information. I've been feeling the same way, but the fears have to be triple for Mom and Dad. I stare into the distance as we enter the Merritt Parkway. Like Cascade Road, it winds and dips. I watch the scenery change as we move into a more populated area.

"Mom, do you think Dad will come home next week?" I ask, sitting up and peering over the front seat.

"Hopefully," she says.

"But you said he is on medicine to stop the infection. How many days will that take?"

"I don't know, Sharon. It will take as long as it takes. Maybe a week or two," my mother replies. "Try not to worry . . . Your father will be home soon."

I nod as I realize that Mom really doesn't know more than what she's telling us. She pulls the car up in front of Mount Vernon Hospital and tells us to get out. I bound out of the car and race David to the trunk. Mom walks to the back of the car to open it. We reach for the balloons at the same time.

"I'll carry them," David says.

I try to snatch the strings from his fists. "They're my birthday balloons!" I snarl.

"These are for Dad."

"Children!" Mom scolds. "This is a hospital."

I back off but fidget with the hem of my dress.

"Wait inside the lobby for me. I'm going to park the car. Best behavior," she adds.

We follow Grandma into the lobby. Panic mounts inside me. Can Dad walk? He'll be so mad if he can't play golf or join us for baseball games this summer. I put the picture together with his white hair. Then it hits me. *Is he old?*

Soon, Mom leads us to Dad's hospital room. I peek around her, looking for him in the bed. Instead, I see Dad sitting in a chair. He is wearing his favorite turquoise bathrobe and look-ing . . . okay, I decide. Relieved, I race into his arms and sob as he holds me close.

"What's up with my birthday girl?" he whispers into my ear.

"I was so scared, Daddy," I say softly, choking back tears. "I thought you were dying and Mom was too afraid to tell us."

"I'm going to be fine," Dad assures me.

I pull away and study his face.

"Sorry about missing your birthday dinner."

"That's all right, Dad," I say. "Besides, we saved my birthday cake until we could all be together. I know all about this dia-betes thing, but can you have a very tiny piece?"

"Wouldn't miss this part of the celebration for anything," Dad says, looking over to David. "Oh, look at the balloons! Come here, son."

"Hi, Dad." David leans in for a kiss without giving up the balloons.

"Are these for me or the birthday girl?"

"They're for us to share," I say.

"I am a blessed man," he says.

Mom and Grandma settle into chairs facing Dad.

"Tell me about your birthday dinner," Dad says.

"It was the best steak ever! Candy spent the night. And you won't believe it . . . but Jackie played pool with me."

"That was generous of him," Dad says, smiling. "How'd you do?"

"I broke the balls wide open . . . even got one into the pocket before Jackie cleaned up."

"Your brother is very good at pool. He should be. Spends most of his free time practicing. Did you play, too, Dave?"

"I almost beat him," David brags.

"He's lying," I say.

"I am not!"

"Okay, we get the point," Mom interrupts.

"How is our favorite horse?" Dad asks.

I look over at Grandma, wondering if she's kept my secret. "Well, I had a little accident yesterday. Got some work to do with him."

Dad chuckles. "When I was in the army, I rode horses. They

can be tricky. Like life, a horse ride doesn't always go the way you want it to go."

For now at least, it seems like my dad is still my dad. I am so relieved, and I enjoy the rest of my birthday with my family, minus Jackie. If only we could all be together again. Wherever he is, I just hope he is safe.

CHAPTER 7

"Segregation now, segregation tomorrow, segregation forever!" George Wallace, the newly elected governor of Alabama, proclaims on national television.

"Did he just declare war?" I ask. Mom and I are watching the six o'clock news in the family room, the evening of the day after my birthday. Usually the space is warm and cozy, but staring into George Wallace's cold eyes, I am filled with fear.

"George Wallace was elected because of his stance on segregation," Mom says.

Elected because of his stance on segregation, I think. People voted for him because he supports these things.

Mom sees the look on my face. "There are people fighting for change as well. In Alabama and all over the country. Reverend Fred Shuttlesworth led a boycott with some college students of the segregated stores in downtown Birmingham at the end of last year. Martin Luther King Jr. and the Southern Christian Leadership Conference have gone there to help organize desegregation initiatives."

"I've heard of Dr. King!"

"Yes, Sharon, he helped plan that dinner honoring your father being elected into the Baseball Hall of Fame last year, even though he couldn't attend. But we go even further back than that. A few years ago, your father and Dr. King were honored by Howard University. Your dad and Dr. King have been in touch ever since, working on marches and voter-registration rallies together."

"Do you think Dr. King will help in Birmingham?"

"Yes, I do. Eight years ago, Dr. King was asked to help organize a bus boycott in Montgomery that led to the end of legal segregation on public buses there. Now he's hoping to achieve similar things in Birmingham. There's a plan to force downtown businesses to open up to Negroes as consumers and workers. The schools also need to desegregate. And until that happens, there will most likely be boycotts, marches, and sit-ins. They will be peaceful, but your father says that some demonstrators may be sent to jail."

I think about the words "segregation forever" and how they sound like a war cry. "Will there be guns and bombs, too?" I jump up and start pacing around our living room as I try to figure out what all this means.

"That's a possibility," Mom admits. "Sharon, come sit down next to me." Mom pats the cushion next to her. I sit back down on the edge of the sofa. She reaches for my hands and rubs the tension from them. "You know that churches have been bombed, right?"

I sniffle. "Sure. Didn't Dad help raise money to repair some of them?"

"He did," Mom says, wrapping an arm around me. "Bombing churches is one of the ways segregationists threaten the protest movement. It happened in Birmingham last month. Reverend Shuttlesworth's Bethel Baptist Church was bombed a day after Dr. King visited Birmingham. And that wasn't the first time it's been bombed."

Thinking about bombs being set off makes my heart race. "Sounds like war to me," I say. I pull away and stand again.

"We have to fight back against oppression, but we share Dr. King's commitment to change through nonviolent protest. There will be protest marches in the streets of cities and towns in the South to help force President Kennedy and Congress to pass laws protecting the freedom of all its citizens. The National Association for the Advancement of Colored People has lawyers fighting cases of discrimination in courtrooms throughout America. And we have the Fourteenth Amendment to the Constitution, which promises equal protection under the law, on our side. Now we need the states to follow those laws."

"That's some army," Grandma says as she walks into the room. She puts her arm around my shoulder to calm me.

"Army," I say, rubbing sweat off my hands and trying to slow my heartbeat. I am still not convinced that there won't be fighting on American soil.

"Honestly, Sharon, it will be a battle. People will get hurt and be put in jail, and some will lose their lives. Dr. King and his followers will remain peaceful, but they are being met with anger and violence. We've seen it plenty of times before. That is the sacrifice people are willing to make so that all Americans will be treated fairly. So that they can overturn the Jim Crow laws in the South."

I've heard about the Jim Crow laws in school and mentioned on the news. They sound terrible. The laws force segregation onto people in public places. There are FOR COLORED signs so Black people know which water fountains, public bathrooms, and even benches are for them. And there are other signs on restaurants and stores that say WHITE ONLY. It makes me mad. They call this "separate but equal." But why should we have to be separate?

Grandma and I sit back down on the couch. Mom continues to look right at me, ready for whatever my next question will be.

"How can they end it?" I ask.

Mom smiles. "One institution at a time. Baseball, the army, public buses—these are all fights that have been won. The Supreme Court ruled in *Brown v. the Board of Education* that school segregation is illegal. Do you remember the students from Little Rock, Arkansas, who desegregated their high school?"

"Of course," I say. There were nine Black students enrolled in an Arkansas high school, but the governor wouldn't let them in. He called the National Guard in to stop them. Even President Eisenhower got involved. "I remember them calling Daddy. He came back to the dinner table impressed by their courage. Wasn't one of the girls named Elizabeth?"

"You were only seven," Mom says. "I'm surprised you remember Elizabeth Eckford."

"Dad showed me Elizabeth's picture in the newspaper. She was walking alone and scared. I can't imagine going to school under that much pressure." The thought of it makes my stomach upset.

"I'll never forget that image either," Mom says. "It wasn't supposed to happen like that. The plan was for all nine students to walk into school together. The date was changed at the last minute, but Elizabeth didn't get the message, so she showed up expecting the others. Elizabeth was mobbed and chased away. She didn't make it into the building that day. A White lady named Grace Lorch helped her onto a bus. Two weeks later, the nine Black students were escorted by US soldiers and finally made it into the school."

"In the picture, Elizabeth was holding her notebooks against her chest," I say.

"For protection," suggests Grandma.

I lean back against the couch and think about the Little Rock Nine. I remembered it differently. In my mind, Elizabeth walked into the building that first day. Now I realize the risks each of the children took, their courage to go forward. I wonder if I'd have the same strength.

"The students were the test case chosen by the NAACP after the Supreme Court's ruling in Brown versus the Board of Education. Proclaiming segregation illegal was only the first step. Someone had to break through and actually attend a formerly segregated school," Mom explains.

"I'm so proud they called Dad. What they did was so important," I say.

"Those students were inspired by his bravery," Mom explains. "It takes courage to be a pioneer and stand up against injustice. Doesn't matter where it happens, on the baseball field, marching in the street, or entering a school that doesn't want you there."

"It makes me so mad that these kids had to go through that just to go to school," I say.

"Your father and I now realize that we didn't prepare you and your brothers for the subtle racism you'd face at your own schools in North Stamford. It took courage for you to walk into your elementary schools knowing you'd be the only Black children. You did it, and each of you fought small battles to survive in those environments."

"But it wasn't the same. Our schools weren't really segregated, were they?" *We live in the North*, I think. *There are no Jim Crow laws here.* But I remember how terrible I felt at Hoyt Elementary School when kids who didn't know me asked stupid and hurtful questions like: "Do you bathe?" and "Why is your skin brown but the palms of your hands white?" They made me feel like I was dirty. It was hard, but we didn't have to walk through an angry mob just to get into our school.

"Actually, Sharon, they are still segregated even if not by law," Mom tells me. "There is discrimination everywhere. Society finds ways to keep the races separate and insecure. The neighborhoods in Stamford are divided by race and income. They have been since before we moved in. When we were looking to move to this neighborhood, we had trouble finding a house that the owner was willing to sell to us. That is called redlining. Real estate agents and property owners in North Stamford had an agreement that the agents would discourage Black families from buying in their part of town. Black neighborhoods were clustered in and around the downtown area. Your father and I saw a number of properties that we wanted to buy. But when we expressed interest, the agents told us they were no longer available. Word got out and my friend Andrea Simon stepped in. She pressured the real estate agents and her neighbors to find us a home. That's how we found this beautiful property on Cascade Road. That was almost ten years ago. It's a little better today, but still this section of Stamford has very few Black families."

"Rippowam is the closest high school to us. I'll be assigned there, right?"

"Well . . . hold on, that hasn't been decided yet," Mom says. "The board of education is working on a desegregation plan for Stamford's three high schools. Remember the goal is to balance out the racial makeup of the high schools. Right now Stamford High School, which is downtown, has the majority of Black students. Rippowam has some diversity, but not enough. In order to reach the racial balance, students will have to be bused. It hasn't been decided yet if the mostly White students who live in our neighborhood will go to Stamford or Rippowam."

"But I'm Black," I say, my voicing rising a bit.

"It will go by zip code. You will be assigned to the same school as our neighbors' children."

"What! Why? What! That's crazy," I protest. "Are you saying

that I may be the only Black kid on a yellow bus bringing White kids to mix with the Black kids at Stamford High?"

"That's about right," Mom says.

I can't wrap my head around that. "Will there be protesters outside my school?"

"I doubt it," Mom tells me. "The school board meetings are open to the public. By the time busing begins, I expect parents will have either bought into the desegregation plan or pulled their kids out of public school altogether. You have that choice, too, you know."

"I don't want to go to private school," I tell her.

David has known only private school education. He goes to New Canaan Country Day School, where he's the only Black student. Most of his classmates are White, rich, and members of segregated country clubs. They pretend to treat all students the same by making them dress alike in blue shirts and light beige pants. But I know that David was bullied about his race—getting into several fistfights until Michael, a popular White classmate, stood up for him. He has good friends at school now, but I bet he still feels like an outsider.

"I want to go to Rippowam because it is a new building. But I'll be okay at Stamford High if I have to go there. At least I'll be in a school with a lot more kids who look like me."

"I hope you won't only make Black friends," Mom says.

"That would defeat the purpose of integration. It's good to make friends with kids from different cultures, religions, and races," Grandma adds.

I immediately think about my friendship with Christy. Even though we still go to church together, we have started pulling away from each other. It's just the way things are, even here. It isn't as simple as changing bus routes. Sure, Black and White students can sit together in class, play on the same sports teams, and go to the same dances. But at the end of the day, they still live separate lives.

CHAPTER 8

Two weeks later, Dad comes home. He's walking with a cane, which adds to my concerns that he's old. He is going to turn forty-four this week, on January 31. Yikes. He is old!

"Where is Jackie?" Dad asks once we've stopped jumping around him, celebrating his return. But someone has obviously been missing from the festivities.

"He left early this morning," Mom replies. I swallow nervously. It scares me when nobody knows where Jackie has gone off to. Anything could happen.

"To go where?"

"Jack, I don't know. Jackie was gone when I got up this morning. He did not go to school. I called some of his friends, but no one knows where he is. I even drove by the pool hall on West Main Street. They haven't seen Jackie in a couple of days."

"Call the bank," Dad suggests.

While Mom makes the call, we try to distract Dad by offering him a piece of Grandma's fried chicken. It doesn't work. In truth, no one has an appetite. We're all too nervous. I nibble on a wing. David starts on a leg. Dad plays with the chicken breast. All eyes shift to Mom as she returns to the dining room table.

"I spoke with the bank manager," she begins. "Jackie withdrew all the money in his savings account yesterday afternoon." *That can't be good*, I think.

"Without our permission?" Dad questions.

"It was in his name, Jack. He didn't need our permission," Mom explains.

There is no doubt that Jackie ran away. By seven o'clock that night, we get confirmation. Jackie and a friend from school got on a bus heading to California. I go to my room and sob. I suppose we all saw it coming. The question is, could we have done more? I'm sure my parents are asking themselves the same thing. I know they tried therapy and putting Jackie in both public and private schools, but he kept spiraling.

Before bedtime, Dad and Mom stop by my room and find me curled up on my bed, reading.

"How're you doing?" Mom asks, sitting down on the edge of my comforter. Dad stands beside her with one hand resting on his cane.

"Worried," I reply.

"We're all worried," Dad says, and settles down on the edge of my bed next to Mom. "Your mother and I hope the boys agree to turn back around. If they go all the way to California, we've arranged for them to stay with Aunt Willamae. My sister has a way with teens. Maybe she can reach Jackie."

"Aunt Willamae will probably drive them back cross-country in her van," I say, thinking of the many summer trips she'd made cross-country with a van load of our Pasadena cousins.

"We'll get him home. Now it's time to get some rest," Mom says, leaning over and kissing me on my forehead. She gets up to leave.

"Good night, Mom," I say. I look over at Dad, happy that he's staying with me. We haven't had a second to talk since he's come home from the hospital.

"Your mother tells me that you saw the news clip from Governor Wallace's inaugural speech," he says.

"It was scary," I tell him.

"Wish I'd been here so we could have talked about it then."

"Mom said that he didn't declare war, but I'm pretty sure he did. What do you think?"

"Well . . . war is usually defined as armed conflict on both sides, but in a way you're correct. We're technically fighting back against segregationists like Governor Wallace. His declaration that segregation will be with us forever makes the challenge real. I hear from the leaders of the movement from all over that people are fired up and ready to march for freedom."

That surprises me. "But aren't Black people already free?" I ask him.

"Guess it depends on how you define freedom," Dad replies. "We're not enslaved, but Jim Crow laws, discrimination, segregation, redlining, sneaky ways to keep Black folks from voting . . . those are all ways to deny Negroes full rights as American citizens," Dad explains. "But freedom is a state of mind, too, Sharon. How do you define freedom?"

I hesitate while thinking about his question. It's the first time anyone has asked me to define freedom. "I know that it's the opposite of slavery or jail," I begin. "But to me it's the way I feel when Diamond and I are galloping. I feel happy. Tall. Like nothing and nobody can stop me. It's fun and exciting at the same time."

Dad beams down at me. "Great analogy, Shar. I used to feel the same way when I'd steal home during a game. Now I feel it on a rare good golf day. I feel invincible. That is one kind of freedom. The civil rights movement is demanding a more lasting form of freedom. We are demanding rights that are legitimately ours because we're Americans. We want to be treated with respect and be free to live in a neighborhood of our choosing, to vote without fear or restrictions, to eat in any restaurant, and shop in stores without first having to walk past humiliating signs. Simple things, too, like being free to enjoy a day at the park with our families. These are rights that most Americans take for granted but are denied to a portion of the population simply because of the color of their skin. It's that basic."

"I get it now, Dad. I'd really like to go on one of those marches and sing freedom songs."

"Why is that so important to you?"

"Because stuck up here in Connecticut, I feel left out of the movement . . . like no one appreciates that we're fighting for respect, too."

Dad leans over and hugs me tight. "You're a special child, Sharon. We'll have to find a way for your voice to be heard. Let me think on that, but right now you better get to sleep."

"Okay, Dad. I love you."

"I love you, too, Sharon. You are so precious to me. Hold that close to your heart. Okay?"

"Sure will. Good night."

"Don't forget to say your prayers," Dad reminds me as he walks out of my room.

I get out of bed and down on my knees. I close my eyes and lean my chin against clasped hands.

"Our Father, which art in heaven, Hallowed be they name . . ." As I recite the Lord's Prayer, I think about Jackie, wishing he was asleep in the bedroom next to David. I'm scared and wish Jackie would call so I can tell him how much I love him. I haven't said those words to him in a long time. Now I regret it.

"God bless Mom. God bless Dad. And God, please bring my big brother home soon."

I climb back into bed and slither deep under the covers.

CHAPTER 9

The next day, Jackie calls from Texas! He's okay but running out of money. I sit so close to Mom that I can hear Jackie's voice. She offers to wire him money to come home. Dad gives Jackie Aunt Willamae's phone number and says she's expecting his call. Before Jackie hangs up, Mom hands me the phone.

"Jackie, I love you. Please come home quick," I plead, so happy to hear his voice. While he drives me crazy with worry, I adore my big brother.

"Miss you, too, sis. I've got things to do. I'll call from Los Angeles," he tells me.

"Things to do," I repeat over and over. What does a sixteen-year-old have to do except go to high school?

Two days later, more news. It's Dad's birthday, but with Jackie gone, we don't have our normal big family celebration.

Jackie calls to say they've reached California and are looking for work picking fruit.

At first, I laugh picturing my brother climbing up a ladder to pick oranges and grapefruit off the trees. But the more I think about it, I get angry and very tired. I go to bed early that night. Before sleep, I say a quick prayer.

"Dear God, forgive my brother. He is a ditz. He hurt Mom and Dad and keeps the rest of us worried. But he is not a farmer. Jackie won't even pick weeds at home. So please make him come home."

The next day, I fall asleep in English class. Even though I went to bed early the night before, I kept having nightmares. I was too busy worrying about my brother. A classmate pokes me in the ribs and I jump up. The whole class laughs at me, and my teacher sends me to the nurse's office.

"What's going on?" the school nurse asks me.

"I'm . . . having trouble sleeping," I stammer.

"Do you know why?"

I nod. "My brother's run away from home," I say between heavy sobs. "He's in California, and my whole family's upset."

The nurse stays with me until I fall asleep on a little cot in the corner of the room. When I wake up, my grandmother is standing over me.

"Grandma!" I say, startled. "What are you doing here?"

"Came to pick you up," she replies.

"I'm going home?"

"That's right. Let's go." We don't talk much until we're in the car.

"Jackie has two loving parents," Grandma reminds me once we're driving away from school. "True, they're at their wits' end trying to find a way to help your brother. But Jackie's their responsibility. It's okay to be supportive, but somehow you have to keep your role straight. Be a good loving sister without sacrificing your sleep, schoolwork, and general health. Right now, all three are in jeopardy. It's time for you to take a step back."

"He's my brother," I say, holding back tears. "I can't be good when he's in trouble."

"I understand, Sharon. Jackie is coming home," Grandma says. "Your mother called just before the nurse phoned. She spoke with your brother and sent him the money to get back."

"What else did he say?"

"He couldn't find a job. Had no money. You can imagine."

"Did he say why he ran away?"

"Actually, he did," Grandma says. "Said he loved us, but he left to find out if he could make it on his own."

"He's only sixteen," I say, feeling anger build.

"I think he knows the limitations now. This trip will help, but it doesn't solve his problems. Sharon, do you know what helps keep my stress down?"

"No."

"I knit. And knit some more," she replies with a chuckle. "How'd you like for me to teach you to knit?"

"I'd love it!" My grandmother knits the most beautiful clothes and sweaters. I can't wait to get started.

* * *

The day before my first lesson, we go to the sewing and knitting store on Main Street. With my grandmother's help, I select a medium-weight wool blend sky blue yarn and needles to match. Then I find a second, soft yellow color so I can make stripes. That evening after dinner, the lesson begins.

"Knitting is a way to use yarn to create a pattern. It's an art done by hand, using two needles and yarn that is looped over them," she tells me.

Grandma has long beautiful fingers and deep polished nails. I sit cross-legged in the middle of her full-size bed. She's sitting on the edge with her body facing me. The skein of yarn is in her lap. Grandma must have noticed me staring at her hands because she comments on them. "It's a family trait," she says.

"What is?" I ask.

"Beautiful long fingers."

I look down at my own hands and notice for the first time their resemblance to my grandmother's.

"We're meant to play the piano," Grandma tells me, glancing down at her watch. "That's what my mother used to say. By the way, we'll miss *Young Dr. Malone* today."

"How come?"

"At first, knitting takes concentration. Once you get good at it, you'll be able to knit anywhere, even while watching our television program. Don't worry, the story lines on that show move like one of your turtles. We'll pick it up in a couple of days. You ready?" Grandma asks.

"Oh yeah," I reply.

"Before we can cast the yarn onto the needle, we need to roll this long skein into a ball. We'll do that together. Hold out your arms."

I stretch them straight toward her. She slides the oblong band of yarn over my arms. "Okay. Open your arms so that the band is taut." She smiles. "Keep the length but relax your shoulders and elbows. I'm going to unravel the yarn into a ball to make it easier to work with."

It takes about five minutes. I drop my arms and marvel at the neat tight ball.

"Now we can cast the yarn onto the needle and begin to make stitches. What do you want to make?"

My heart pounds out its excitement. "Can I make a sweater?"

Grandma chuckles. "Eventually. For now, we need to make

a piece that's straight. It will be easier for you to learn the basic stitches."

"I could use a warm scarf," I suggest.

"Perfect. Let's make that the first project."

Grandma picks up a tape measure and we decide the scarf's width and length. "We'll cast on enough stitches to give us the width we want. I'll show you, then you can take over."

I scoot in closer and watch as Grandma knots the yarn onto a needle and begins the looping process. The yarn is wrapped around the index finger of her right hand and somehow my grandmother lifts the yarn off the finger so that it loops over the tip of the needle point.

"Wow," I say as I lean over to get a better view and try to figure out the move.

"Flip your legs around and sit beside me," Grandma instructs. I move in from the middle and dangle my legs over the side of the bed. "Closer." I inch over until our hips are practically locked and then Grandma hands me the knitting needles. "Doing is the only way to learn this craft," she says.

We spend the next two hours painstakingly looping yarn onto the needle and then ripping it all out.

"Well, now you know, knitting isn't easy," Grandma says, patting my thigh. "Make this row perfect."

Perfect means that each loop looks the same as the one next

to it. My fingers ache at the joints and at the tip of my index finger where the needle point keeps jabbing it.

"Shake them out," Grandma suggests.

I drop the needles in my lap and shake my hands about, then pick the needles up again. After three loops, I smile over at Grandma. "Think I have it now," I say with confidence.

"That's my girl."

Grandma gets up from the bed and leaves the room. I sit there focused on the yarn and knitting needles until I cast on enough yarn for the scarf. I check each stitch. Then I hop up and jump about the room. "Grandma," I shout, "I did it!"

The next day, Grandma and I spend all of Saturday continuing my knitting lessons. I learn the basic knit stitch quickly, so she throws in the purl stitch. My fingers pick up speed as I complete a couple of rows, alternating a row of knit with one of purl. By the middle of the week, I can almost work without making an error and not be too distracted by the drama on our hospital soap opera. My scarf measures twelve inches on the day Jackie gets home.

CHAPTER 10

Jackie's return takes me by surprise. I get off the bus and walk a short distance home from the bus stop and open the door. He is grinning down at me from the top of the steps.

"Hey, sis," he says, like it's a normal day.

"Jackie!" I shout as I drop my books and race into his arms, sobbing like an idiot.

"I'm fine, Sharon," he says, patting me on my back.

"Don't you ever run away again," I scold between sobs.

"I'll have to leave someday, you know," my brother tells me.

"Not until you're eighteen. And not without letting us know long before you leave," I tell him.

"How about seventeen?" he teases, pushing me away and looking down.

I wipe away my tears and smile. The relief is so big it has chased away all the anger. "Wait, how'd you get here anyway?"

"Mom and Dad picked me up at the airport early this morning," Jackie says. "We drove back to Stamford. Dad dropped me and Mom home and then headed into the city for a meeting. Mom should be home soon. She and Grandma went to the grocery store."

"Oh," I say.

"Dad's steaming," Jackie tells me.

"But he must have been happy to see you, right?"

"In a way," Jackie says. "He didn't have much to say to me. Guess he's really mad."

"Well, he has a right to be. We all do. You scared us. But that's all over. Isn't it?" I pull my brother by the arm into the living room. We fall onto the sofa and sit near each other. I stare into his eyes, trying to see if he's changed.

"I'm back," Jackie says without making any promises.

"I learned how to knit while you were in California," I tell him. "Grandma's teaching me."

"She's the best," Jackie says, touching my cheek.

"I love you so much, Jackie," I tell him as I fight back tears.

"I love you, too, Shar. I hate to make you sad." He pulls me into a hug. "Just take care of yourself and stop worrying about me."

I relax, safe in his arms. "That's why I'm knitting. When I start to worry, I get out my knitting needles." I laugh. "Want to see what I'm making?"

"You bet," Jackie says, moving his arms from around my shoulder.

I stand up and walk casually to my room, wishing life with my big brother was nice like this every day.

* * *

Within a week, I have perfected the basic knit and purl stitches. Grandma and I knit while we watch her favorite soap opera. We have a great afternoon routine going. But I'm aware that Mom, Dad, and Jackie are seeing a psychologist. Jackie is trying to be good. He takes the bus to school each day. I don't know if he spends the whole day at school or if he skips out at lunchtime, but he goes to try and make Mom and Dad happy with him. Jackie's around in the evenings more. He even watches the six o'clock news with us and contributes to our dinner table discussions. He likes to talk about the civil rights movement. Still, it's hard to deny the tension bearing down on us whenever Jackie and Dad are in the same room. It's hard to believe that Jackie will stick around. Our home life is not easy these days, so I bury myself in schoolwork, knitting, and long horseback rides.

It doesn't solve any of the problems, but it does make it easier to get through the day.

CHAPTER 11

In April, Dad and Mom travel to Venezuela for vacation. Dad is still limping and using the cane, but he can manage to get on and off planes. Before Grandma arrived, our parents would hire a sitter to help Willette watch us at home when they traveled. Sometimes that was a disaster. Jackie got rid of a couple of the ladies. I remember one sitter who got so angry with Jackie that she chased him around the house, threatening to throw a can of Hawaiian Punch. David and I watched in horror. That incident got Mom home quick! But now I have no worries about my parents leaving for a week, because Grandma and Willette are home with us.

While they're away, Willette and I discover a love for grape juice with a scoop of vanilla ice cream in it. It hasn't replaced 7-Up with ice cream as our favorite; it just gives us an alternate snack here and there. Most afternoons are the same. I walk home from the bus stop and sit with Willette at the kitchen table. We make our drinks and talk about my day at school. After I'm refreshed, I go down to Grandma's room to knit and watch the hospital soap operas. Grandma's added a new twist in her push for me to become a nurse. She encourages me to marry a doctor. I love this time with her, but I don't feel like I need to worry about my future job or who I will marry yet.

All this is before I help take care of Diamond and do my homework. Surprisingly, David and I divide Diamond's care with almost no problems.

Jackie has stayed enrolled at Rippowam High School and he's still coming home for dinner on school nights. Weekends are a different story. But as long as he makes it home, I'm happy. My parents, of course, want Jackie to stick with the established curfew, so every few weeks, there's a blowup when Jackie's pushed the boundaries too far. All things considered, though, he's doing better.

Now I have new worries. The school dance is getting closer. I hate the whole idea and dread the humiliating experience of standing off to the side, knowing the color of my skin makes me out of bounds for being asked to dance. I've been planning to protest the mandatory attendance but haven't discussed it with my parents yet.

The first Saturday after my parents return from vacation, Dad and I are back to our routine of making weekend pancakes.

"You're flipping them too soon," Dad reminds me as I toss a second mashed-up, half-cooked pancake into the garbage disposal.

"It has bubbles on top," I say.

"Not enough, Sharon. Wait until there are lots of tiny bubbles and a browning along the edge of the pancake, then flip them."

"Dad, I'm not a little girl anymore," I protest. "I know how to make pancakes."

"Then what's the problem?"

He's right, of course. I'm distracted. It's been happening a lot lately. Part of me wants to tell Dad about the stuff happening at school, but I'm not ready. It's hard standing next to him and not just saying what's on my mind. So I focus on making the best pancakes instead. After two flops, I carefully measure and pour a quarter of a cup of batter onto the warm griddle and hold the spatula at the ready while Dad fries the bacon next to me. My father was the one who taught me how to make pancakes, but now I'm determined to show him that I know what I'm doing. The batter spreads into a perfect circle and bubbles form on the exposed side. I wait until the surface looks like a crater before sliding the spatula under the pancake and twisting my wrist. Perfection!

I glance over at Dad.

He smiles back at me.

Soon he's pulling crispy bacon out of the pan and I have a pile of golden-brown pancakes on a plate.

It's just Dave, Dad, and me this morning. Jackie's still asleep and he only ever eats cold cereal for breakfast anyway. Mom doesn't eat pancakes. She's busy swapping out the winter clothes in her closet for her spring and summer wear. Grandma's visiting her friends in Brooklyn, and Willette has gone home for the weekend.

We sit down and dig in.

"Do you have plans for today?" Dad asks each of us.

"I'm gonna ride Diamond and hang out with Michael this afternoon," David replies as he pours a huge glop of maple syrup onto his plate of pancakes.

Dad turns his questioning eyes to me.

"I have to help Mom clean out my closet. Bor...ing..." I sing out with great drama.

"Let's go into the city this afternoon," Dad suggests, looking only at me.

"What! When? Now?" I yell. I've always loved going into the city with my dad.

"After breakfast," Dad replies. "You can work on your closet next week, with Willette."

I act cool, but I'm bubbly with anticipation.

"I want to come, too," David says.

"This trip's for your sister. I missed her birthday celebration and we need some father-daughter time."

"What are we going to do?"

"Got a few things up my sleeve," Dad replies.

"The city" is Manhattan to us in the Connecticut suburbs. It is the most exciting place in the world. But for Dad and me, our father-daughter excursions into the city are less about the excitement and more about solidifying our bond.

During his baseball-playing days, Dad was constantly traveling. He didn't get to spend as much time at home with the family as he wanted. David and I were young, so we were less affected by his absence than Jackie. It seems to me that's part of the problem with Jackie and Dad today. There's a distance between them that doesn't exist with David and me.

Dad retired from playing baseball in January 1957, just a week before my seventh birthday. He became the vice president of personnel with the New York–based coffee company Chock full o'Nuts. Since then, Dad drives to and from his office on Lexington Avenue each day, getting home in time for dinner on most nights.

He's dedicated to making up for the time he missed out on with us. We take lots of family trips, and he makes it a point to find special activities to do with each of us. The boys love to fish with Dad, either in the lake or someplace where they can get on a boat. Once a year, the whole family goes to Montauk to fish. But Dad and I have made New York City our fun place. Our father-daughter visits began when I was seven. I loved seeing the city through Dad's eyes. It also allowed me to see Dad through other peoples' eyes.

It was always an adventure right from when Dad told me where we were going. Willette and Mom would dress me up. I'd sit beside Dad on the drive into the city as we'd head out along the hilly, curvy Merritt Parkway. Dad has a way of making a simple car trip into a roller coaster ride. As the car would speed up the hill, crest, then dive down again, I'd giggle and hold my belly. It was such fun!

Dad's office is on the floor above a Chock full o'Nuts coffee shop in Midtown Manhattan. As soon as we walked in, every head would turn toward us. From the ladies behind the counter to the cashier and customers ordering food, everyone knew my dad and they had a favorite baseball moment to tell him about! Dad would plant me on one of the twisty counter stools with assurances from the waitresses that they'd keep me entertained. Then he'd head up to his office quickly. It was thrilling to be left alone when I was younger. The women who worked there would feed me rectangular pecan brownies and hot chocolate, then entertain me while I ate. Their eyes sparkled, arms flung about, and fingers snapped as they shared precious memories about seeing my dad play baseball.

"We'd pack a lunch and go to the park right from church . . . still in our Sunday school clothes."

"Once my father and I took the train all the way to Pittsburgh just to see Jackie play. You know that no one since Babe Ruth brought more fans into ballparks."

"Your daddy kept the pitchers guessing while he danced on and off the base. Then, just when the pitcher figured out his rhythm, he'd steal home!"

I went to a few of my father's baseball games, but I was too young to appreciate his talent or the way he excited the fans. Listening and watching these dramatic replays from the women, I began to form a picture of Dad as a baseball player.

By the time Dad walked back into the coffee shop, the place would be rocking with laughter, hand slapping, and foot tapping. Over the course of a few years, everyone got a chance to tell their story. I began to understand the excitement and the hope that Dad brought to the Black community. I'd look over at my dad smiling along with all these people. *He is so important to them*, I would think each time.

At home, we have photographs from Dad's years with the Dodgers and a trophy room with his Most Valuable Player Award, his Silver Bat Award, and lots of signed baseballs. I'd go home after our outings and look at these trophies in a new light.

But these memories told through the voices of Black men

and women were even more special than the trophies and awards. They made it clear that my dad's performance on the field meant many things to many people. There were pure baseball fans who admired his speed, solid batting, and daring to steal home. But for a lot of people, he provided inspiration. To do the impossible. To reach for equality. To be included. If Jackie could do it, so could they. On these trips when I was just a kid, I got to learn who my father was to the world. After that, he was no longer just "Dad" to me.

Then, we'd leave Chock full o'Nuts to go shopping in the wholesale market district. Walking the city streets, we'd hold hands and stop for the fans who called out, "Jackie! Jackie!" It seemed to me that all of New York must have lived in Brooklyn and been fans of the Brooklyn Dodgers. Well, maybe not all of New York. Sometimes Yankees and Giants fans would stop us to recall a memory and ask for an autograph. Dad always made it clear that he was spending time with me and that I was his priority. It made me feel important, protected, and loved.

That message was reinforced in the clothing showrooms of Lower Manhattan. Those were the places where buyers from the big department stores purchased wholesale clothing for their stores. They were generally closed to the public, but Dad was an exception.

The first stop was always 1333 Broadway, where Mr. Love, the famous designer of girls' dresses, housed his incredible junior fashion line. Mr. Love had met Dad at Ebbets Field, and we'd been going to see him ever since. Our annual visit was often followed by seasonal gifts that made all my friends jealous. After being shown around the massive showroom with racks and racks of beautiful dresses, I was overwhelmed by so many choices. Dad would leave it up to me to decide on color and design. We'd leave the warehouse with a box of dresses in lavish colors like periwinkle, pink polka-dot, soft yellow, and, one very special time, a gray-checked dress with a red petticoat.

Usually, our next stop would be to get something for Mom. Dad loved surprising Mom with presents. The sales staff would bring out a dozen negligees and we'd pick out six for Mom. I'd picture my mother looking beautiful in each of them. It was so much fun selecting my favorites. Even then, I thought it was romantic. I dreamed of someday getting married and having babies, my make-believe husband surprising me with gifts like these.

We would always follow up the wonderful shopping with lunch at a nearby restaurant, where I'd complain about ballet or piano lessons or whatever other activity I was growing tired of. That would lead Dad to tell me the story of how Chock full o'Nuts became one of the largest coffee companies in the world, again. I figured the message was that hard work pays off. But it never swayed me into a love for piano or ballet.

Those were all the things I loved about my trips to the city when I was a kid. But now that I'm thirteen and more of a grown-up, I can't help but wonder what our father-daughter days will look like now.

Sure, there's always hair, clothes, and boys, but I have more important things on my mind. I honestly don't know where I fit in anymore. I feel guilty about not being connected to any of the civil rights groups. We don't attend a Black church. And I feel more and more out of place in all-White North Stamford. I'm not sure what to do about these things. It's not just my body that is changing—the world is changing around me. I need Dad to help me figure out how I can be more involved. So I'm thrilled that he wants to take me on one of our father-daughter dates today. My hope is that time alone with him will give me the direction and confidence I need to figure everything out.

CHAPTER 12

We arrive in the city shortly after two. Dad parks uptown in front of one of his favorite Italian restaurants. They're expecting us. The owner and Dad slap each other on the backs and chat as he shows us to our table. We both order veal parmigiana. Our favorite.

"You still haven't told me where we're going today," I say while I lay my napkin across my lap and look around the restaurant.

"I want to keep it as a surprise," Dad says, trying to bring me back to him. "Mostly, I wanted us to have some time alone to talk. What's new, Shar?"

I take a sip of iced tea and twirl the glass around. I have no idea where to begin before lifting my eyes to meet Dad's. "I feel different."

"To be expected," Dad replies, eyebrows raised. "Tell me about it."

"Everyone talks about changing hormones, moods, and things like dancing and going out on dates. All that's good, but I'm interested in understanding other things. It's like I'm seeing everything around me differently than I used to."

"Can you give me an example?" Dad suggests as he leans in closer.

"I don't seem to fit in anywhere," I tell him.

Dad jerks up in his chair. "What do you mean?"

"Dad, did you know I wouldn't wear my glasses in elementary school because I hated having one more thing that made me different?"

Dad shakes his head. "No, first I'm hearing about that."

"Or that I was teased about my skin color and asked if I took baths. The kids made me feel dirty. I was so shy back then, I wanted to disappear. Not be noticed," I say.

I can tell Dad's shocked into silence. I want to go on, but I'm starving, so I cut the veal into pieces and hum with pleasure at the first bite. Dad takes my cue and dives into his veal parmigiana as well.

I wolf down chunks of meat and twist strands of spaghetti around my fork. "It's good, right?"

"Why didn't you tell me before what was happening at Hoyt?" Dad asks after our initial hunger has been satisfied.

"It didn't seem important," I reply, swallowing half a glass of iced tea. My eyes jerk up when Dad drops his fork onto the plate.

"How can you say that, Sharon?"

"Dad, come on . . . We talk about the civil rights movement a lot. With all that is happening, it would be ridiculous for me to whine about silly White kids calling me names," I say.

"But you're talking about several years back. Why didn't you tell us about the name-calling then?" Dad asks.

I shrug my shoulders. "I didn't have the words," I admit. "Back then, we were talking about the Little Rock Nine. How brave they were. Believe me, I felt that way about them, too. But it kind of makes what was going on in our schools seem trivial. I just wanted to make you and Mom proud." I pause to think about what I want to say, then continue. "I'm just now starting to face up to how much it hurt. And it wasn't until I heard Governor Wallace speak earlier this year that I really thought about how mean some White people are to Blacks. I was glad when Mom explained the difference between segregation in the South and what we have up here. That's why I'm telling you now. I'm just beginning to feel like I have the words, beginning to understand the issues of race in this country."

"Makes me feel bad," Dad says while signaling to the waiters to remove the plates. "We should have spent more time talking about what you and your brothers were experiencing. Tell me what's going on with you at Dolan?"

He catches me off guard. I'm still thinking about what he's just said. *Was Dad right? Could we have been better prepared for our own experiences? Why was I so shy in elementary school?* "I don't want to go to the school dance," I confess.

"Why not?"

"It's embarrassing, Dad," I say. "It's okay to play touch football with White boys, but they won't ask me to dance."

"You mean because you're Black," Dad finishes my thought.

"That's right. Seems there's a line that's drawn and we're not supposed to cross it."

"We saw the same thing with Jackie when he became a teenager," Dad admits. "That's why your mother signed up you and David for Jack and Jill. Is the dance in the evening?"

"It's during school hours. That's the problem. Attendance is mandatory."

"I think you should go," Dad says. "You have to face these sensitive issues of race. Going sends the message that you deserve to be there ... and you do. Don't let anyone else define your value, Sharon. You don't have to fit in. Stand out. Be the best you can be. Don't wait for anyone to ask you to dance. Dance with your girlfriends. Dance alone. Just dance."

Dad puts money on the table to pay the bill. Then he looks

over at me. He can see the serious expression on my face. "Let's get out of here and have some fun."

I perk up. "Fun? Where are we going?"

"To the Apollo Theater."

My head practically spins around. "What! You mean the Apollo where all the famous singers and bands perform?"

"That's right," Dad says, grinning big. "My friends Peter and Bobby are waiting for you. They've arranged for you to go backstage to meet Little Stevie Wonder before he performs."

"What!" I can't believe it. I'm going to my first concert at the Apollo Theater and I get to meet one of my favorite singers! Wait till I tell Willette and Candy!

The Apollo Theater is on 125th Street between Seventh and Eighth Avenues. The security person opens the side door, greets Dad and me, then walks us upstairs to see Dad's friend Bobby Schiffman, the manager of the Apollo. Peter Long, who promotes a lot of big concerts, joins us, and I watch Dad come to life in a totally different way. In seconds, he is laughing and slapping his knees while everyone tells their stories. When it's time, Peter takes Dad and me downstairs to the holding area outside the changing rooms.

Within minutes, Stevie Wonder walks through the door and greets us.

"Hello, sister," he says to me.

"Hello," I reply shyly.

"This is my daughter's thirteenth birthday present," Dad tells Stevie.

"I'll be thirteen next month," he says to me.

I nod.

"Ready to have some fun tonight?" he asks me.

"It's my first live concert," I reply.

"Then let's get it going."

Dad and I are ushered to seats in the second row, center. The place is packed and loud! Fans are clapping and calling for the show to begin. I am mesmerized. The velvet curtains are drawn, revealing a piano with microphones, drums, and a music stand.

Stevie Wonder walks onstage blowing his harmonica. We go wild! I stay on my feet, totally immersed in the music. Stevie performs for a solid hour. When he sings "When You Wish Upon a Star," I think he's singing just for me.

CHAPTER 13

"May I have your attention, please?" The announcement from Mr. Moon, our principal, booms over the loudspeaker. "A number of students have approached me to be excused from the school dance. So I want to clarify the rules. Two weeks from Thursday, the entire eighth grade is to report to the gym at one fifteen p.m. The dance will be over at three, in time for regular dismissal. There will be a sheet to sign in and out. Make sure you check in with your homeroom teacher. They will have the sheet. Two weeks to go. Be excited, students! The staff and student committee has worked to make this a fun time for all."

I'm in homeroom organizing my papers and books for the school day. I listen closely to Mr. Moon's remarks and think: *He didn't absolutely say we couldn't appeal that decision. Did he?* I sense my request will be denied, but I'm going for it.

When the bell rings, I drift out of homeroom and head to math class. The hallways are crowded. I pass clusters of girls chatting excitedly about the dance and what they will wear. I hurry on, wishing it was a shared joy.

The next day, I stop off at the office before first period and make an appointment to see Mr. Moon. Then I spend the homeroom period outlining my concerns about the dance.

Dad says that you build confidence with success. I had success the first time I appealed to Mr. Moon. That was a year ago for a different kind of issue. In Stamford, junior high school goes from seventh to ninth grade. Within each grade, the students are divided into nine groups. One is the highest and nine is lowest. Candy and Christy are in the top group. But because I scored poorly on a junior high school entrance exam, I was placed in group seven.

I was embarrassed by the low group but hadn't thought about ways to move up until I learned that students had to be in groups one through four to take a foreign language. I wanted to take Spanish in eighth grade. I went to Mr. Moon to ask that my status be reviewed. During the discussion, I told him that I needed to take a foreign language to get into college. That I was a good student who needed to be challenged. I argued that a single test score should not limit my future. He promised to review the matter with my teachers. Before we parted,

Mr. Moon asked me why I was so adamant about specifically taking Spanish.

"I saw *West Side Story* and got inspired," I said, thinking of Natalie Wood and Richard Beymer singing together.

"I loved the movie as well. But what about the story piqued your interest in learning Spanish?" Mr. Moon asked.

"I know that it's a modern *Romeo and Juliet* with singing and dancing. A Puerto Rican girl and a White boy fall in love, but the rest of the people in the gangs around them don't want them to be together," I explained. "Maria's story is like mine. She's different and not sure where she fits in. She's looking for her place in the world. I feel that way, too."

On my final seventh-grade report card, I learned that I was promoted to group four for eighth grade. Unfortunately, Spanish wasn't offered, so I chose to take French instead.

Now I'm back with a new request. *Will Mr. Moon agree this is legit or will he think I'm being silly?*

"How are your classes this year?" Mr. Moon asks when I sit down across from him.

"They're fine," I reply while trying to maintain eye contact. I am very nervous, which makes me think I have a weak case. "I couldn't take Spanish because it wasn't offered, so I'm taking French and trying to get my grades to a B," I say, referencing the incident from last year.

"Is that why you're here?"

"Oh no. I want to speak with you about the school dance," I say. "I know you said attendance is mandatory."

"Did you hear my announcement this morning?" he asks.

"Yes, but I feel that students who object for personal or religious reasons should be given another option. We could help out in the office or—"

"Sharon," Mr. Moon interrupts. "Junior high is a difficult transition for most students. Girls and boys are often shy around one another. The dance is one way to begin to break through that in a nonthreatening environment."

Is the school dance nonthreatening? I'm not sure. It was a threat to my sense of myself. But I don't say any of that.

"The only way we'll get beyond the discomfort is to get to know the other students," Mr. Moon continues. "I know you have a lot of friends here at Dolan. Perhaps you can dance with them in groups? That will ease the shyness and fears of being a wallflower. Sharon, we have to confront our insecurities and learn how to manage in the larger world. You may surprise yourself and have fun."

I'm still not sure about it, but since my dad wants me to try it and so does my principal, I'll give it my best shot. I stand up and shake Mr. Moon's hand. "I'll be there."

CHAPTER 14

There's no school the next day. It's Good Friday. Only Mom, Dad, and I are home this weekend. Jackie's in New York City with his friend Bradley Gordon, and David's spending the night over at Michael's. I wake up to find that Dad has already left to play golf. And Mom's doing paperwork at the kitchen table.

I ride Diamond to my friend Cindy's house. She lives up the hill near our church and is the only other person on Cascade Road with a horse. Sometimes we ride together. Her horse is a tall palomino. Side by side, our horses look like the cartoon characters Mutt and Jeff. Diamond may be smaller, but he's strong and fast.

Cindy's waiting for me when I arrive. "My dad set up a jump in the field next door. I was heading over to give it a try. Want to come along?" Cindy asks me as she tightens the saddle straps.

"Would love to," I say, patting Diamond on his neck.

"Glad you put a saddle on Diamond. Dad's strict about safety," Cindy tells me. "Let me tell him that you're coming along."

I'm not sure how to take her comment. My parents are strict on safety, too. They also know that I've been well trained and generally have good judgment. During the winter months, I admittedly prefer to ride Diamond without a saddle. His belly is round and he has a thick winter coat that keeps him warm, cushions my butt and legs, and allows me to have a good grip.

I hop off Diamond and grab his reins. "I'll hold the horses while you get your father," I say, and Cindy hands me her reins.

"Be right back," she says.

Cindy and I have jumped our horses before. But they were always low jumps on the dirt road. We created them from tree branches and bricks found near a building site. I'm excited to see how Diamond will do with a real jump.

Cindy comes back out with her dad. He waves from the open doorway. "Good morning, Sharon. I'll meet you and Cindy in the field."

We walk our horses from the driveway to the open field adjacent to the house. Cindy rides with an Eastern saddle and claims it gives a smoother ride then a Western one. Personally, I like to ride Western with its horn on top.

We stop and study the jumps while we wait for her father.

The first one is so low that the horses can walk over it. The second one is higher. We'll have to canter right up to the jump, then urge our horses over it.

When Cindy's dad arrives, he coaches us, "As you approach, lean forward with your back straight. All the weight should be on your heels. Keep the reins loose. It's okay to hold on to the mane."

I've been trained in jumping but have very little actual experience and an unpredictable horse. I lean over and whisper to him, "We can do this." I direct Diamond over to the first jump.

"That's it. Walk him up to it. He'll naturally step over the fence."

I look back at Cindy. "You go first," she says.

I urge Diamond forward and, as predicted, he steps over the low fence. Cindy follows me on her horse. We repeat this action several times, rewarding our horses with carrots when they perform.

"The next jump is more challenging. You'll have to canter up and over. Warm the horses up and then go for it."

We ride the horses around the field in preparation before lining them up a distance from the jump. Cindy goes first this time. I watch as she and her horse gracefully lift over the jump. When it's my turn, I tap Diamond with my heels, make a kiss sound with my lips, and we're off. As we approach the jump, I can feel Diamond's front end lift as I tilt my pelvis forward.

"Good job, Diamond. Good boy." I praise him repeatedly and slide a carrot into his mouth. Cindy cheers and takes her horse over the jump a second time. We're excited and yelling words of encouragement to each other as we keep practicing our jumps.

After we're finished, I say, "That was so much fun!" I walk Diamond around the field so he can cool off.

"Want to come inside for a pop?" Cindy asks.

"No, thanks," I say. "I've got to go home." I'm anxious to get back and report our success to Mom.

"Congratulations, girls. Great start today. I've got to go, too. Happy to spot you both anytime," Cindy's dad says before walking up the steps of their front porch.

I race home, excited to share my big news.

"Mom," I call out right as I'm through our front door. I take off my boots and leave them in the closet. As I enter the living room, I hear Dad talking on the phone. It's an intense conversation. I head back to my parents' bedroom and find Mom reading the *New York Times* on the screened porch off the bedroom. "I jumped Diamond today!" I happily report.

Mom drops the paper to her lap and looks up at me. She smiles. "I didn't know you went out to jump Diamond. Sit down and start from the beginning."

I sink into the cushioned teak chair across from Mom and give her a blow-by-blow account. "It wasn't the first time I'd jumped a horse." I remind her about the training I'd had before Diamond came to live with us. "Mom, it was so cool. Diamond was amazing. He didn't hesitate."

"Because he knows and trusts you," Mom tells me. "You and David have really turned this horse around. I'm so proud of you both."

I beam at her. "We love him, Mom. Sure, he acts out sometimes, but he's also a lot of fun."

"Just promise me you'll be careful. Jumping can be dangerous. Safety has to be on your mind at all times," Mom tells me.

"I was riding Diamond with a saddle," I say, feeling a little defensive.

"Well . . . that's something. I'm glad Cindy's dad has agreed to spot you and Cindy. That's important," Mom says.

"So what's up with Dad?" I ask. "He sounds really mad."

"Some trouble in Birmingham," Mom says. "Dr. King was arrested today. He's in jail."

I'm shocked. I know the police were arresting marchers, but I assumed Dr. King would be safe. "Is he all right?"

"I guess so. Your father will tell us more when he's off the phone," she replies.

"I'm off," Dad says as he walks through the door, looking worried. "And the news is troubling."

CHAPTER 15

"Dr. King, Ralph Abernathy, and Fred Shuttlesworth are in solitary confinement, so no one's allowed to visit them in jail," Dad tells us after he sits down.

"But why were they arrested?" I ask, feeling annoyed that the police arrested Dr. King and insulted him further by putting him in solitary confinement.

"They were arrested for disobeying a court ruling forbidding protest marches," Dad says.

"When will they release him? Today?" Mom asks.

I look back over at Dad anxiously. This is big news and I'm trying to figure out what it all means.

"Doesn't sound like it," Dad tells Mom. "I'm afraid the local authorities want to make this as difficult as they can for the men."

"Isn't Birmingham in Alabama, where that mean governor lives?" I ask as I try to understand what's going on.

"That's correct," Dad says. "Dr. King is there to help out the local leaders, like Reverend Shuttlesworth, who leads a group called the Alabama Christian Movement for Human Rights. Earlier this year, Dr. King, Reverend Shuttlesworth, Reverend Abernathy, Reverend Wyatt Tee Walker, and Reverend Andrew Young met to discuss a campaign to end segregation in downtown Birmingham. All the men are members of the Southern Christian Leadership Conference. I joined Martin last year in Birmingham to speak at an SCLC dinner. Martin considers Birmingham the most segregated city in the United States. With good reason. The Black churches there have been bombed so much they call the city Bombingham. Reverend Shuttlesworth's church alone has been bombed three times. It's terrible."

Hearing about the bombs terrifies me. How can people be so cruel? "It sounds to me like Negroes are being forced to stay in a tiny corner of the city. How are they supposed to survive?" I look to Dad for answers.

"There are plenty of Negro-owned businesses. That's how the Negro community has survived. There are small grocery stores, restaurants, churches, newspapers, funeral homes," Dad explains.

"Oh," I say. It reminds me of Stamford's West Side, with its Black hair salon, barbershop, pool hall, and schools where the classrooms and hallways are filled with Black students. Negroes can walk into a White beauty shop in downtown Stamford, but they'll be told, "We don't do Black hair."

"That's the way it is throughout the South. Blacks and Whites are kept separated by laws and customs. And it's wrong. That's why the civil rights movement is so important," Dad says. "That's also why Dr. King chose to have his demonstration on Good Friday. He's hoping to spread the word and get national attention for the crisis in race relations throughout the South."

"To force Americans to understand how bad things really are," Mom adds.

"Dr. King and Reverend Abernathy knew the television crews would be on top of this story. The images of them being hauled off to jail on Good Friday could be what we need to turn the nation around," my dad explains.

"Jack, tell Sharon what Dr. King is trying to accomplish in Birmingham. It's important," Mom says.

"You're right, Rae. The goal is to desegregate businesses in downtown Birmingham," Dad tells us. "There are other demands. Important ones, like getting a committee together to work out school desegregation. So far, they have been ignored. Black people still cannot eat at lunch counters there in the downtown area."

I picture myself being told that I can't get a milkshake at the soda fountain. I'd be mad! It just isn't right.

The phone rings in the middle of our conversation. Dad rushes off to answer it.

"This is a lot to take in," Mom says to me. "How does it make you feel?"

"Not sure," I admit. "Mad and sad at the same time. I wouldn't want to live like that."

"For most of the families, the southern way is the only life they've known. Many do leave. Your other grandmother, Mallie, is one of those brave people. When her husband left her, Mallie moved your father and his sister and brothers across the country to Pasadena, California, and made a new life for them," Mom explains. "That was over thirty-five years ago and the conditions in the South have not changed. The civil rights movement is our hope to break down segregation and give Negroes full rights as citizens."

"Like the right to vote," I say, trying to hold back a yawn.

"You're tired," Mom says. "Why don't you go shower and find something quiet to do in your room. I think your father will be on and off the phone for the rest of the day."

"Okay, Mom," I say as I stand up and stretch.

"Glad you had such a good day with Diamond."

"Yeah, thanks." With all the news from Birmingham, it suddenly seems unimportant.

I turn back and ask one last question. "They're calling Dad to get his advice, right?"

"Yes," Mom tells me. "Your father has been an activist all his life."

"That's so cool," I say. "Dad is pretty important to people, isn't he?"

"Someday, you should ask him about that. Now, go get a warm shower and practice your flute or read," Mom suggests.

"Love you, Mom."

"Love you, too, Sharon."

* * *

On Easter morning, I leave home early for sunrise service with our Sunday school class. It's warm and sunny. Our teacher walks us to a cleared gathering spot in the woods next to the church. We stand in a circle as the sun rises and pray together. During silent prayer, I think of Dr. King locked away in a cold, dark jail cell. I wonder what he's doing on this sacred morning.

Thinking about Dr. King's courage, I step forward when selected to read the Twenty-Third Psalm. "This is for Dr. Martin Luther King Jr.," I tell my classmates. "He's in a Birmingham jail today. Arrested for leading a protest march for freedom." I clear my throat and start to read: "The Lord is my shepherd; I shall not want. He maketh me to lie down in green pastures:

he leadeth me beside the still waters. He restoreth my soul: he leadeth me in the paths of righteousness for his name's sake. Yea, though I walk through the valley of the shadow of death, I will fear no evil: for thou art with me; thy rod and thy staff they comfort me. Thou preparest a table before me in the presence of mine enemies: thou anointest my head with oil; my cup runneth over. Surely goodness and mercy shall follow me all the days of my life: and I will dwell in the house of the Lord forever."

I step back, feeling good about myself for recognizing Dr. King. I wonder if he's written a special sermon for this Easter morning. Or maybe he'll recite King David's Twenty-Third Psalm softly to himself. While I read the words, I think of Dr. King as the shepherd. Strengthened by his love for God, he has led thousands of men, women, and children. They've marched beside him, shown up to hear him speak, and are willing to sacrifice their own freedom so that others will have it. They are the faithful. The believers. I open my eyes in this peaceful setting, feeling refreshed as our teacher leads us in singing "Christ the Lord Is Risen Today."

CHAPTER 16

A week later, Candy and I attend the spring meeting of the Stamford-Norwalk chapter of Jack and Jill. They meet regularly to discuss current events and do community service. The organization promotes education and leadership in the Black community. They also host dances and fund-raisers with other chapters, but I haven't been to one yet. Mom and Dad enrolled me so I could meet other Black children my age.

It's a warm Saturday morning. Fifteen kids are crammed into Mrs. Dickerson's living room in a midrise in downtown Stamford.

I'm dressed in black stirrup pants and an off-white pullover knit sweater, hoping I look more like a teenager. Candy and I huddle together on the couch in the Dickersons' living room. We're still finding our way with this group of kids.

After welcoming the group, Mrs. Dickerson asks us to go around the room and reintroduce ourselves. When it's my turn, I stand up reluctantly and say my name. "I'm Sharon Robinson. I turned thirteen in January. I'm an eighth-grade student at Dolan Junior High." I look around, sensing that most of the others are in high school. "My favorite things to do are play the flute and horseback ride. I have two brothers, Jackie and David. Some of you might know my older brother, Jackie, from Rippowam. My mom and dad both work in New York City. My grandmother is teaching me how to knit. I'm excited about the spring Jack and Jill dance, but not my eighth-grade class dance. I don't want to go to it." I stop abruptly and consider sitting down, but I notice a hand. "Yes," I respond, surprised that there's a question.

"Why don't you want to go to the dance at your school?"

I look at the boy while I try to find the right words. "It's going to be awkward," I tell him. "Candy and I are the only two Black girls in the school. There's one Black boy, who we don't really know. I don't want to be holding up the wall for an hour and a half while everyone else has fun around us." I drop down onto the couch before anyone else asks a question. The kids clap. Candy speaks next, echoing my concerns. She's followed by our friend Twanda, who's a couple of years older than us.

"Don't worry," Twanda says. "Parties are always awkward at

first. It'll get better," she tells us before introducing herself to the group.

I like Twanda and am happy that she didn't put Candy and me down as silly kids. Twanda's different from most of the others. She's an only child who lives with her father. I don't know the whole story, but her mother doesn't live with her anymore. Maybe that's why she's nice to us, because she knows about Candy's mother.

After all the introductions, Mrs. Dickerson stands up again and starts the meeting with current events. She calls on a boy I don't know.

"Dr. King's in jail in Birmingham, Alabama," he reports, then settles back down on the floor. It's a small living room without enough seats for all the kids. Some are squeezed onto the two couches, a few others are in the dining room chairs, and the rest are sitting on the living room rug.

My heartbeat quickens. I look around, feeling hopeful that we'll get into a conversation about Birmingham and Dr. King. I'd love to know what other kids think of the movement.

"My husband, Nate, and I have friends in Birmingham. We called them Easter weekend to hear more about Dr. King's arrest." Mrs. Dickerson has picked up the conversation. "We got confirmation that Dr. Martin Luther King, Ralph Abernathy, and Fred Shuttlesworth were all arrested on Good Friday. The friends also told us that on April twelfth, the same day as the arrest, the Birmingham newspaper published a statement written by eight well-known White Alabama clergymen."

I sit up straight and lean toward Mrs. Dickerson so I won't miss a word. This is news to me. *What did they say?*

"The men represented different faiths: two Episcopalians, two Methodists, a Roman Catholic, a Jewish rabbi, a Presbyterian, and a Baptist. They called for the Black community to reject Dr. King's marches," Mrs. Dickerson tells us.

I'm stunned. *Why?* I wonder.

Mrs. Dickerson bends down to pick up a stack of papers from the dining room table. "I made copies of the newspaper clip. Who wants to volunteer to help me read it?"

I raise my hand and am picked along with Mrs. Dickerson's daughter Natalie and the boy who brought up Dr. King in the first place.

Mrs. Dickerson reads the first paragraph. I stand next to her, listening and reading along at the same time. It seems to me that the clergymen agree that there are racial problems in Birmingham. They expect the Black community to wait on the courts to end segregation. The language in the second paragraph is hard to understand. "What does 'forbearance' mean?" I ask Mrs. Dickerson.

"Patience. Self-control," she tells us.

"I thought so," I say.

In the next paragraph, the clergymen refer to Dr. King as an outsider. They also write that the demonstrations are unwise and untimely. I drop my right hand and let the letter dangle. I've read enough. This is the most frustrating piece of nonsense I've heard in a long time.

Mrs. Dickerson takes over and reads on.

I sit back down, too angry to stand in front of the others another second. I can feel the tension building around me and know others feel the same way. Some fidget. A couple kids get up and head to the bathroom. Others mumble in a low growl, half-hoping their anger will be heard.

I remember how Dad described life in Birmingham for the Negro community. Haven't they suffered long enough? Why shouldn't they demonstrate? Dr. King and the others led peaceful marches. He is not in Birmingham to incite anyone. He is there to show the world how bad things are. To show the world what segregation really means for Black Americans.

Mrs. Dickerson opens the floor for discussion.

"Why is Dr. King the target if he was asked to help?" a girl who looks a bit older than me asks.

"Good question," Mrs. Dickerson says. "The ministers who wrote this letter have been working toward racial justice in Birmingham since January. They're partially motivated by the fear that their efforts will be seen as ineffective. Their reputation is on the line, too."

I'm still upset from the letter. I raise my hand and when Mrs. Dickerson calls on me, I tell everyone about life in Birmingham and how my dad raises money for the movement. The more the kids in the room listen to me, the more I smile and nod my head. *This must be what it feels like to be in high school*, I think, proud to be a teenager.

"Doesn't the Constitution give American citizens the right to protest and speak out against injustice?" Natalie asks.

"Sure does," a girl shouts from the back of the room. "It's the First Amendment. Freedom of speech and the right to assemble peacefully. It's all written in the Constitution."

The sense of rebellion in the room is exciting.

"Let's hear it for the First Amendment," someone calls out. The group bursts into applause. I stand up to clap harder, loving the energy and thoughtfulness of my new friends. *Jack and Jill isn't only about parties*, I think.

The consensus in the room is that the White ministers are wrong. Dr. King, Ralph Abernathy, and Fred Shuttlesworth have the right to direct and lead protests in the streets.

"We'll break now for lunch but will continue this discussion at the next meeting," Mrs. Dickerson tells us. "During that time, please watch the news and read newspapers. You can all go to the Stamford library to read the national newspapers as well as the local ones. Let's see if the Negro community agrees with the White ministers to stop protesting, or if the marches continue and grow. We'll also see how Dr. King responds."

After a lunch of small tuna and chicken salad sandwiches, the meeting agenda turns to the upcoming Jack and Jill dance. It's scheduled for the first Saturday in May. It will be held at a club in downtown Stamford. Mrs. Dickerson reports that with the other Jack and Jill chapters coming, she thinks that a hundred young people will be in attendance. We go over what's expected of us, things about proper dance behavior, that make me want to giggle. Several kids report on refreshments, music, and decorations. I like how thoroughly the members have planned the event and think that I'd like to join one of the ongoing committees. We wrap up the discussion with dress code.

I lean over to Candy. "What's semiformal?" I whisper to her.

"Party dress," she tells me. "Don't worry. Aunt Billie will know what to do. But first we have to get through the awful school dance."

"Don't remind me," I groan. "It's this Thursday."

I don't want to think about it. I'd rather concentrate on being with my new Jack and Jill friends.

CHAPTER 17

Thursday morning, I wake up in a cold sweat. *What's there to be nervous about?* I say to myself. *Just go to school, show up at the dance, have some fun, then get on the bus to come back home.* I scold myself. It's no big deal. *Dr. King just spent eight days in jail and I'm worried about a dance? No way, Sharon.*

I get up and put on my plaid dress, knee-high socks, and white Keds sneakers. I know that most of the girls are dressing up in something special. I want to protest, so I purposely dress casual. I check myself out in the full-length mirror and smile. *This is not a party dress*, I think. It's subtle. I brush my hair, pull it back, and clip it so that it lies neatly at the nape of my neck. In the kitchen, Jackie hands me the box of Rice Krispies while he pours milk onto his cereal.

"Isn't today the school dance?" he asks, looking me up and down.

"Yep," I say.

"Shouldn't you be wearing stockings? You know, try to dress up."

"I am pretty just like this," I tell Jackie. "I don't need to dress up to prove it. Besides, I'm not dancing," I say, covering my cereal with milk and joining the rest of the family at the table.

Mom and Dad are talking about their days while David loudly slurps the milk from his bowl. Mom spots me and smiles. "You look cute," she says. "But what about wearing tights with that dress and your Sunday school flats?"

I sigh and start eating my cereal. "I'm okay like this."

"I see," Mom says, sounding exasperated. "Sharon, this is a class activity. Like it or not, you're part of this class. Stop acting like they've singled you out to insult you."

I look up. Mom has a point, but I can't give in.

"Even if the dance is mandatory, the dress code isn't."

"You can dress as you please, but I expect you to be polite and act like you're having fun even if you'd rather be somewhere else," Mom says.

I get it. I really do. "Okay," I agree.

"Just remember, dancing is not a spectator sport," Dad tells me. "Get on the dance floor and move those feet. Do the two-step. Or, what's that crazy dance I see you kids doing? The Twist, isn't it?"

My dad, Jackie Robinson; my brother Jackie Jr.;
my mom, Rachel Robinson; and me as a baby

In the backyard of my first home in St. Albans, Queens, New York

When my younger brother, David, was born, we moved to Stamford, Connecticut.

Family time at the house was very important to us.

Awards and plaques celebrating my dad's achievements on and off the baseball field fill the walls of his trophy room. Dad broke Major League Baseball's color barrier by joining the Brooklyn Dodgers in 1947. He led them to a World Series win in 1955.

In 1957, my dad announced his retirement from baseball. We all attended the special events commemorating his career. My grandma, Zellee Isum, attended this one with us.

After retiring, Dad spent more time at home with the family.

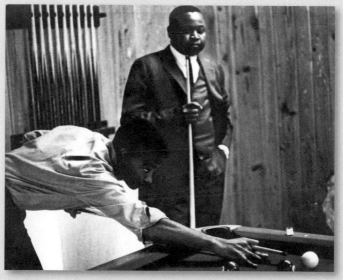

Jackie Jr. loved shooting pool at our house with friends.

Me and my best friend, Candy Allen, in 1963

At Jones Beach: Carolyn Grant (Aunt Billie's daughter), me, Candy, and Kimberly Allen (Candy's sister)

My ninth-grade class photo from Dolan Middle School in Stamford, Connecticut. Candy is second and I'm sixth from the left in the front row.

My brother David, me, and my friend Christy Joyce, skiing.

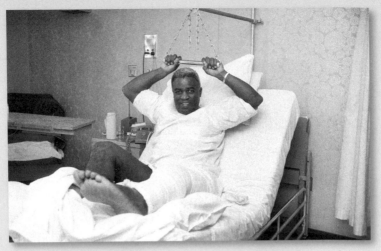

My dad recuperating from his knee surgery days before my thirteenth birthday.

After retiring from the Dodgers, Dad worked as vice president of personnel at Chock full o'Nuts in New York City.

As part of his activism, Dad frequently worked with Dr. Martin Luther King Jr. Dad spent his post-baseball years traveling the country raising money for the civil rights movement.

In May 1963, Dad traveled to Birmingham, Alabama. He was greeted by Reverend Wyatt Tee Walker (second from left) of the Southern Christian Leadership Conference. Boxing heavyweight champion Floyd Patterson (third from left) also made the trip there.

Floyd Patterson, Reverend Ralph Abernathy, Dr. Martin Luther King Jr., and Dad met about the rising unrest within Birmingham.

Floyd Patterson and Dad survey the damage at the A. G. Gaston Motel bombing, one of many in a series to hit the southern city.

Dad speaking at the New Pilgrim Baptist Church, Birmingham.

David and my father at the March on Washington in August 1963

I fainted from the heat and the large crowd, but David and Dad marched on. Mom, Jackie Jr., and I met up with them in time to hear Dr. King's "I Have a Dream" speech.

In September 1963, we held our second jazz concert fund-raiser at our house in Stamford, Connecticut. Some people rowed their boats over to listen to the music.

My mom and dad confer with our special guests, Dr. Martin Luther King Jr. and Roy Wilkins, head of the National Association for the Advancement of Colored People (NAACP). Marian Logan and Dr. Arthur Logan stand in the background.

David played a drum as I received a flute lesson from jazz legend Herbie Mann while Dad and Mom looked on.

Mom and Dad were so proud to raise money for the cause.

Me as a young adult and my dad. His legacy of activism is always with me.

"Don't let them back you against the wall waiting to be asked to dance," Jackie says. "You've got a bunch of girlfriends. Get together and have fun."

"Are you really saying this to me? Do you ever participate in school activities?" I tease.

"Don't be like me, sis," he replies, walking away from the table.

"You can also do the Mashed Potato," David suggests as he jumps out of his seat to dance. He wiggles his feet, just about making me crack up.

"All right, I give up. I'll change my attitude and have some fun," I concede.

"Seriously, sweetheart, I remember when you were too shy to speak up in class. I like that you're standing up for yourself. Just choose your battles wisely. Our goal is full access even when we don't feel like we fit in. Once inside, we make our own party," my dad says.

* * *

Five hours later, I stroll into the gym as "Surfin' U.S.A." by the Beach Boys pulsates through large speakers. The normally bland gym is decked out in balloons and streamers. It's not my favorite song, but it makes me smile. Students are moving around the room, but no one is dancing. I find Candy standing near the punch bowl, talking with a few girls.

"Let's get this party started," I challenge the girls right as the DJ, who is actually my social studies teacher, puts on Chubby Checkers's "The Twist." Kids hear the familiar beat and pile onto the dance floor.

I pull Candy into the middle like Jackie had done with me last year when this song and dance craze topped the charts for the second time. "The Twist" hit number one in 1960 and then again in 1962. It was the first song to do that two separate times. Jackie taught me how to do the dance, and we had a ball. Now Candy and I swivel our hips and arms to the music until the song ends.

"Contract on Love" by Stevie Wonder comes on next, and I think of my surprise trip to the Apollo and seeing Stevie perform this tune in person. When "I Will Follow Him" by Little Peggy March starts up, the entire class heads to the dance floor.

We dance until we're sweaty. Girls take off their pumps and dance in stocking feet. I bounce around comfortably in sneakers. I'm glad I was stubborn about wearing comfortable clothes earlier today. As I look around, I realize I was worried that all the other kids would be in couples and I'd be alone. But it doesn't look like that now. We're all still just kids playing together in the gym. I'm not sure what the next few years will bring, but for now, it is party season and I have two big ones back-to-back, so I keep dancing.

CHAPTER 18

That weekend, Aunt Billie shows up at our house with Candy in tow. Her theatrical entrance thrills me.

Aunt Billie is Candy's father's sister, and my mother's dear friend. But under her stage name, Billie Allen is an actress, dancer, and entertainer. She was one of the first Black actors to appear on television both as a recurring character on a television show and in commercials. I remember going to see Aunt Billie in a Broadway play called *Critic's Choice* three years ago. It was amazing to see her onstage with Henry Fonda and Georgann Johnson. Sometimes she reminds me of Rosalind Russell in the movie *Auntie Mame*. Everything about her is terribly exciting to us.

I giggle as she tosses her long black raincoat onto our white sofa. It lands draped over the edge exactly in the right spot and Billie is free to wrap her arms around me. I sink into her embrace, feeling relief that Candy's cool aunt has come to our rescue.

"Sharon . . . darling," Billie sings out as we snuggle.

Mom floats into the living room and hugs Billie while Candy and I spread out across the floor and chat. There is no mention of the school dance. I figure Mom and Aunt Billie have agreed to leave that in the past. It is time to focus on our first Jack and Jill dance. Candy and I have filled them in on the first meeting and they hope the dance will produce similar good feelings about the organization.

"The invitation says semiformal, and you know those Jack and Jill girls don't play," Aunt Billie says. "They like to look sharp. Which means we need to go shopping!"

"Where are we going?" I ask.

"Bloomingdale's, of course," Billie tells us.

Aunt Billie drives Candy and me into town, entertaining us along the way with funny stories about her children, Dwayne and Caroline. Once we get through Bloomingdale's front doors, we trail behind her like she's the Pied Piper of Hamelin luring us to self-confidence with her magical personality. In the teen department, we try on every party dress we see. Candy wears a size seven but has to pick a dress to fit her five foot, nine-inch height. I'm five foot five. My legs feel too long, but they're not nearly as long as Candy's. It takes us some time, but finally Candy picks a white cotton pique dress with huge blue flowers and I choose a soft yellow one with a full skirt. We twirl around the fitting room, giggling and admiring ourselves in the mirror.

"Perfect!" Aunt Billie sings as we venture outside the dressing room to a public viewing. "You both look so beautiful!"

I doubt we look beautiful. I look over at Candy and back into the mirror at myself, thinking: *We're awkward. Lanky. Nervous. We both wear glasses. And our legs are out of proportion to our bodies.*

My mother and Candy's aunt are both beautiful. But with Billie's assurance, I decide there's hope for us. I stand taller.

"Now, take those dresses off so we can find shoes and get to the restaurant before they stop serving lunch," Billie says as we scurry back into the dressing room to change.

Over lunch, Billie brings up the fact that Candy's dad is getting married in a few months. I realize that this is a tender subject for my best friend, so I stay quiet. Her dad is marrying into Detroit's elite. His bride-to-be, Gail Burton, is a psychiatrist. Candy told me that there's a ballroom in Gail's parents' home. I can't even imagine it.

"We need to talk about the Jack and Jill dance," Aunt Billie says, getting back to our shopping trip and much-anticipated party. "I'm coming as a chaperone."

We scream for joy. If my mother or Candy's dad had said they were going to be chaperones, the reaction would be different. But Billie will help make the night fun and less frightening. Billie's children are members of a chapter of Jack and Jill on Long Island, where they live. She's a big fan of the organization.

"I'm glad you like the idea," Billie says as we linger after the plates have been cleared.

"You're my cool aunt," Candy reminds her.

"Well, I may not be so cool if you girls don't dance," Aunt Billie says. "You have to keep in mind that most teenage boys are shy. They're afraid of being turned down. It's safer for them to keep a distance. As they get older, that changes. It's okay for you to do the asking or for all the girls to dance together. Just get on the floor and have fun."

Gee, I think. *Not this lecture again. Why didn't the adults just let us find all this out for ourselves?*

"If you're too shy," Billie continues, "I may send the boys your way."

"What!" I protest, now realizing the downside to having Billie as a chaperone.

"Aunt Billie, that would be so embarrassing," Candy says, leaning back in her chair.

"Humiliating," I add as I wave my arms about, to emphasize the point. "You don't need to hold our hands. Please let us figure this stuff out."

"Okay, then . . . make sure you don't spend the whole dance off to the side."

"Do we have to wear our glasses?" Candy asks.

"Can you see without them?"

We both stare straight at Aunt Billie, trying to decide how to answer that question.

"I can see shapes, not faces," I confess.

"About the same with me," Candy says.

"Well, then, you've answered your own question."

* * *

The morning of the dance, Mom brings Candy and me to the only Black hair salon in town. It's packed with customers and has the usual smells of chemicals and frying hair. I sit down and watch a girl get her curly hair straightened with the hot comb, then curled under with a curling iron. The hairdresser misses and the hot iron grazes the girl's ear. She shouts at the hairdresser and I flinch, remembering when it happened to me. This is one of the reasons why I talked Mom into getting my hair relaxed today. The chemicals used in the relaxers can do damage to hair, but the straightening process lasts much longer then a weekly hot comb.

When it's my turn, I climb up into the tall seat and watch the hairdresser grease my scalp and then apply the white crème relaxer. The second it starts to burn, we rush to the sink to wash it out of my hair. I'm relieved when it's over. My straight hair is set with curlers, and then I sit under the hot dryer.

I pull out my copy of the book *Stormy, Misty's Foal* by Marguerite Henry. The children's librarian at the downtown public library recommended it to me. She knows all about my adventures with Diamond and thought I'd enjoy reading about the Chincoteague Ponies. Misty, the mare character, is about to give birth to her foal when a terrible storm hits Virginia and complicates things. I'm in the midst of reading about the winds and rain and a frightened Misty when the hairdresser comes to tell me my hair is dry. I shut the book, hating to be interrupted just when the action is kicking in. But I'm immediately happy when I see my hair with bangs and gentle shoulder-length curls. Candy and I stare at each other and start laughing.

"I like it," Candy tells me.

"Me, too. I like yours, too."

"Your hair looks great, girls," Mom says when she arrives and we pile into the back seat.

"Thanks, Mom. I'm starving," I reply, leaning up against the front seat.

"It took three miserable hours," Candy complains as she collapses into the seat like she's faint.

"This should help," Mom tells us, then hands me a paper bag with chips and ham sandwiches.

We dig in, mumbling our thanks between bites.

North Stamford is a thirty-minute drive from the west side of town. After Mom drops Candy at her home off Scofield Road, we head home. Once I'm back in my room, I look at the clock and realize more than half the day is over. It is a real process getting ready for this dance, but Candy and I want to look extra nice for our Jack and Jill friends.

Billie is picking me up at six thirty. I dance about the room with mounting excitement. Ever since attending that first Jack and Jill meeting, I've felt completely different about this party. It helps that I already know and like some of the girls and boys. Sure, I have the jitters. Who wouldn't? It's one thing to dance in the safety of your bedroom. It's another thing to dance with two hundred eyes staring at you. And a chaperone who's monitoring your behavior. But then I think about how I made it through the school dance and even managed to have some fun dancing with Candy there, and I relax a little bit. I take my new dress out of the closet and hang it in full view of my bed. I lie down. *Will I look pretty in it tonight?* I wonder.

* * *

The dance is being held at a community center in downtown Stamford. Candy, Billie, and I walk in to the sounds of Martha and the Vandellas. This was one of the most fun songs to groove to at my school dance!

Billie goes to check in with the grown-ups, so we separate from her to go looking for familiar faces. "I Want a Love I Can See" by the Temptations has me humming along as we wander around the room. I'm immediately drawn into the Motown music, the sounds of laughter, and several couples dancing in the middle of the room. I see a few faces from our Jack and Jill chapter meeting and wave in their direction. Then I spot our friends Twanda and Natalie standing in a circle of friends from Rippowam High School. I'm impressed with the way they're dressed. High school looks so sophisticated!

Twanda waves us over. Candy and I have on dresses with full skirts that touch our knees and we're wearing flats. Twanda's dress is fitted and she's wearing high heels. *Someday*, I remind myself, *I'll be old enough to wear heels*.

"You girls look great!" Twanda says with her usual warmth.

"So do you," I reply.

"This is Linda and Barbara Smith." Natalie introduces us to the two girls with them.

"I'm in your brother Jackie's class," Linda tells me as we shake hands. "Is he coming tonight?"

"No," I say, wondering what she'll say about Jackie. "He's not a member of Jack and Jill."

"My sister has a crush on him," Barbara adds when we greet each other.

Oh no, I think. *Why does she think I want to know that?* If Jackie is going to be the center of this whole conversation, I'm not staying.

"All the girls crush on your handsome brother," Linda says.

My eyes roll around and I want to sink through the floor. This is embarrassing.

"Speaking of love, how's our favorite dentist?" Twanda asks. Candy's father is the dentist for a lot of the kids we know. "And when's this fancy wedding everyone's talking about?"

"This summer . . . I think," Candy replies, keeping it vague.

"I'm thirsty," I say, hoping to break up this gossip session before it gets any more personal. "Want to get some punch?"

"Love to," Candy replies.

"Sharon, please find my mother. She has something important to tell you," Natalie says before we move off.

"Okay," I say, waving goodbye and heading toward Mrs. Dickerson. We greet her.

"Sharon, you were especially active in our discussion about this at the meeting. I wanted you to know that Dr. King has written a formal reply to the letter from the clergymen," Mrs. Dickerson tells me.

"Really?!" I say. I'm curious and pleased that she wanted to share this information with me. "Thanks for letting me know. I'll ask my father about it tomorrow."

"Good. Have fun tonight, girls," Mrs. Dickerson says.

As we walk away, I'm thinking about Martin Luther King Jr. He and Ralph Abernathy stayed in jail for eight days. I wonder how many of those days were in solitary confinement and when he had a chance to write. I knew they were back to work in Birmingham and, hopefully, would not go back to jail any time soon.

As Candy and I move on toward the punch bowl, the music and dancing draw me back into a party mood. I really hope I get to dance.

Marvin Gaye's "Stubborn Kind of Fellow" starts up, and it reminds me of dancing with Candy on my birthday. I smile at her.

We hum and sip punch in between notes. The dance floor is hopping. Kids pump their hands in the air and call out, "yeah, yeah, yeah," when prompted by Marvin Gaye. It's fun being in this lively room filled with brown-skinned folks. My feet move as I look longingly at the dance floor. I am giving myself a pep talk when I look over and see Aunt Billie waving over two cute boys. They bend down to hear her, then look up in our direction. I'm mortified!

One of the boys starts to walk over to me. My legs are shaking. My mouth is dry. I can't look him in the eye. *Did Aunt Billie tell him to come get me?* I worry. He stops an arm's distance away from me.

"Would you like to dance?" he asks after he's finally crossed the room.

"Sure," I reply, trying to act calm while my heart is racing. We head to the dance floor.

The Ray Charles record "Take These Chains from My Heart" is playing. I know the words. Candy is right behind me. I want to ask her if this is considered slow dance music, but there's no opportunity.

I look down to see how the boy's feet move. He takes my right hand in his and rests his left hand gently on my waist, guiding me into a two-step. I think of my dad's advice. The dancing isn't bad. At least we're not tripping over each other's feet. My arms relax and I stop focusing on our feet.

"I'm John," he says when my eyes lift to meet his.

I look up at his kind face and smile. "My name's Sharon. Did Billie tell you to ask me to dance?"

He chuckles. "Honestly, I wanted to ask you to dance anyway. Your friend just gave me permission."

"That's nice of you. I still feel embarrassed," I say, looking away from John.

"Don't be. Is this your first Jack and Jill dance?" John asks.

"Isn't it obvious?" I reply with a nervous laugh. I think John is older than me, so I ask him, "Are you in high school?"

John nods. "A freshman at Rippowam. What about you?"

"I go to Dolan," I say.

He is a nice polite boy, I think to myself while we sway to the end of the song. I drop my arms, assuming the dance is over. John picks up my hand and our movements shift from slow to up tempo as "Baby Workout" by Jackie Wilson pumps through the speakers. John twirls me around and I giggle for so long that he eventually joins in. When the song winds down, John and I stroll off the dance floor and then turn to each other. "Thank you for dancing with me, Sharon," he says, shaking my sweaty hands. "Hope to see you around."

My heart pounds happily. I look down at my pointed-toe flats, grateful that they made contact with the middle of the dance floor. Then I look over to where Billie's sitting and catch her wink at me. I send her back a wide grin.

CHAPTER 19

The next morning, David jumps on my bed with news. "Dr. King wrote Dad a letter."

I bolt upright. "What did it say?" I ask.

"I don't know," David admits. "It was early in the morning and Dad was in a rush. He's playing golf now but should be home by one. Said he'd show it to us then. Hey, what time did you get home from the dance?"

"Eleven thirty, I think," I say, glancing over at the clock beside my bed. "It's ten thirty now?!"

"Yep. You never sleep this late. You must have danced a lot," David says.

"Twice with the same boy," I report with pride. "It was a fun party. I'll be right back," I say as I hop out of bed, grab my bathrobe, and run to the pink bathroom attached to my room.

When I come out a few minutes later, David is lying across my bed. "Something's odd," I say. "Last night Mrs. Dickerson told me that Dr. King wrote a letter from jail. I bet that's the letter Dad's talking about."

David shrugs. "Maybe. Is Dr. King still in jail?"

"No, he's been out a week," I say, and scoot my brother off my bed so I can make it. "If Dr. King did write to Dad, he probably wants him to come to Birmingham."

David stares at me with doubtful eyes. "Did a boy really ask you to dance?"

I toss a pillow at his head. David ducks so it lands on the floor. "Let's go find Mom. Maybe she'll know more about the letter. Come on," I say, sliding my arms into my bathrobe. "I'll race you."

We almost knock each other over trying to get out of my bedroom door at the same time. I crack up and force my way around David. We're both laughing so hard we collide into the walls.

"Won," I say, tagging the door to the kitchen.

"Good morning, Sharon," Mom calls from the kitchen table, opposite the sink.

I look over and see her sitting next to Jackie. "Morning, Mom. Jackie. Can't believe you woke up before me this morning," I say to my brother.

"Hey, sister. Must have been a swinging party," Jackie says, and finishes the last of his breakfast.

"Sure was," I report. I pick up a piece of cooked bacon from a plate on the stove.

"Why don't you make scrambled eggs to go with that?" Mom suggests.

"All I want is a slice of toast," I tell Mom, slipping bread into the toaster. "Thanks for saving a few pieces of bacon for me," I say, carrying my plate and pulling out a chair with my other hand. David slides down onto the chair beside me.

"So what happened?" Jackie asks.

"We had fun. A couple of girls asked about you. Did you know that Linda likes you?"

Jackie shrugs his shoulders. "So?"

"It was so embarrassing, Jackie. Really. They told me that all the girls crush on you," I tell him. "At least now we know you go to school," I say with a chuckle.

"Don't start anything, Sharon," Mom warns.

"I'm not," I say as I hold a piece of bacon in the air. "Actually, I hated the gossip and refused to stay and listen to it. Why do girls talk so much about other people?"

"Not just girls," Jackie tells me.

"Really?" I hadn't heard either of my brothers gossip. "What do boys gossip about?"

"Girls," Jackie says, laughing.

"Did you and Candy dance?" Mom asks me as she looks sternly from Jackie to me.

"We did. I danced with a boy named John. He's a freshman at Rippowam. Funny thing is, Billie had something to do with that," I tell them.

"You mean Billie got some boy to ask you to dance?" Jackie says, shaking his head and laughing at me.

"We danced two times." I gulp down a glass of orange juice. "John told me that he wanted to ask me before Billie called him over. But he needed the push. I guess boys really are shy, too." I am about to ask Mom about the letter from Dr. King when Dad walks in, dressed in his golf slacks.

"Hi, honey. We were just catching up on Sharon's big night," Mom says, getting up and greeting Dad with a kiss.

"You won't believe it, Dad, but the two-step came in handy," I report.

Dad laughs and walks over to the stove to pinch off a piece of bacon. "Glad to hear that. Must have been a nice young man."

"He was very polite and respectful," I say. "Dad, what's this about a letter from Dr. King? Did he write it to you?"

"Not to me," Dad corrects. "Dr. King wrote it from jail to a group of White clergy who publicly criticized him. I made you copies so we could read Dr. King's response together. Let me get them."

We all sit together in the living room, filling up the sofa and sprawling across the big leather chair next to the fireplace. The floor-to-ceiling windows allow the sun to flood the room. Jackie, David, and I have questions for Dad. Dad reminds us that Dr. King and the SCLC were invited to Birmingham by Reverend Shuttlesworth and other local leaders. "So the premise of the letter from the clergy is incorrect. They made it sound like Dr. King was an uninvited crasher. Here, start to read it to yourselves. It's a long letter," he warns, handing us each a stapled copy. "I'm going to change out of my golf clothes. Be back shortly."

After our parents leave the room, I curl up on the sofa with the papers in my hands. David is sprawled out on the carpet below me, and Jackie is lying with his legs looped over the arms of the leather chair. We've only been reading for about five minutes when David interrupts us.

"I can't believe Dr. King wrote this whole letter while he was in jail. Where'd he get the paper?" David asks.

"He must have had some paper in his jacket pocket," Jackie suggests.

"Or maybe the guards gave him a piece of paper and a pencil." It strikes me that maybe this was the sermon I'd imagined him writing on Easter morning. Flipping through the pages, I, too, wonder where he'd gotten this much paper.

"Maybe," David agrees, then finds another problem. "But wouldn't a pencil be considered a weapon?"

Even Jackie laughs while we come up with all kinds of theories on how Dr. King found enough paper to write a long sermon. Our loud laughter brings Dad. "I didn't find anything funny in the letter," he says, stepping down into the living room.

"We were laughing with David," I say, still chuckling. "Wasn't Dr. King in solitary confinement?"

Dad settles down on the sofa beside me. "He was. Why?"

"Well . . . we were wondering where he got the paper and pencil. Did the guards give it to him?" David asks.

"That's actually a good question," Dad replies. "It came up during my conversation with one of Dr. King's organizers, Wyatt Tee Walker."

"So this Wyatt Walker man gave Dr. King the paper?" David asks. We are beginning to fidget, waiting for a simple response. Dad seems ready to tell us an entire story.

"Not exactly," Dad replies. "At first, Dr. King wasn't allowed to make any calls or have visitors. When he was moved out of solitary, someone snuck in a copy of the newspaper that contained the public statement written by the clergymen. Do you know about that statement?"

"We read it out loud at our Jack and Jill meeting," I tell him. "They called Dr. King an outsider who was stirring up trouble."

"Well said, Sharon," Dad says.

"I haven't read it," Jackie replies.

"Me either," David says.

"On April tenth," Dad tells us, "the city of Birmingham signed a temporary ordinance prohibiting Reverend Walker or anyone associated with him from sponsoring or participating in demonstrations or parading without a permit. Two days later, King and Abernathy went through with a previously scheduled protest and were arrested. Eight prominent White clergy published a statement in the local paper urging people not to participate in mass demonstrations sponsored by outsiders. The clergymen accused Dr. King of using extreme measures. Dr. King read the letter and immediately started making notes along the margins of the newspaper and on scraps of paper from his pockets. When his lawyer visited, he brought Dr. King the pads of paper he'd requested."

"This letter is too hard for me to read," David complains.

"Dad, I'm trying to read it, but I don't understand parts of it either," I say, pointing out the sentence that begins with "We are caught in an inescapable network of mutuality, tied in a single garment of destiny."

Dad nods. "Birmingham is one of the most racially

segregated cities in the nation. It has a history of oppression. Dr. King writes of police brutality, unjust courts, and the unsolved bombings of homes and churches owned by Negroes as examples. When Dr. King writes 'the inescapable network of mutuality,' he's saying that all communities are connected by racial injustice and what affects one community affects the rest of the country. He goes on to explain the goals of the Birmingham campaign and the civil rights movement in general. Does that make sense?"

"Yes," I reply. Then I read on.

"Dr. King is warning White people that if they reject his nonviolent strategy, this could push some in the Black community to try other strategies. Dr. King writes that he agrees that the demonstrations do increase the tension. But he says that tension will force negotiations. There is an urgency," Dad says.

"As a Black man, I feel that tension everywhere I go. I'm tired of being watched like a criminal. King's right. The situation is urgent," Jackie says, slapping the rolled letter against his shin, then unrolling it and flipping through the pages. "Like King says: 'freedom is never voluntarily given by the oppressor; it must be demanded by the oppressed.'"

It's the first time I've heard him admit he's angry. I'm beginning to understand why. We live in the same household, but Jackie spends most of his time downtown in the

Black community. His experiences are very different from my protected world. In my head, I repeat Dr. King's words about freedom and the oppressor. The governor of Alabama comes to my mind. I will never forget George Wallace's words or his hatred toward Black people. I close my eyes, trying to shut out his cold expression. Instead, I hear his words repeated over and over: "Segregation forever." I feel like I need to do something to fight this, but I don't know where to start.

I'm only vaguely aware that Dad and Jackie are talking about the anger in the Black community. Dad agrees with Jackie that it's not just in the Deep South. It's across America. I notice that David is quiet, taking it all in like I am. Then I hear my name. "Are you all right, Sharon?"

My eyes burst open. "I guess so . . . Just thinking about Governor Wallace on television so I know how an oppressor looks and talks."

"If my history teacher brought this letter in for discussion instead of having us memorize a bunch of facts and dates, his class would be so much more interesting," Jackie says.

"Why don't you bring Dr. King's letter in and read it to the class?" Dad suggests.

"No," Jackie says without hesitation.

Dad presses Jackie to reconsider. "It's unusual for Dr. King to respond to people who criticize him, which makes this letter historic from many perspectives. Your history teacher should be open to a class discussion on it. If you take the initiative, you might get extra credit."

Maybe I'll do that, I think.

Jackie shakes his head and lifts up from the chair. David jumps up, too. "Want to go fishing?" he asks Jackie.

"Let's do it,"' Jackie replies.

We thank Dad for bringing home the letter and head out.

CHAPTER 20

Over the next two weeks, Jackie, David, and I speak with Dad daily about Birmingham. We use what we're learning to write school papers. We go to the public library to do research on Dr. Martin Luther King and Birmingham. Dad helps out by bringing us home articles on Birmingham from the New York newspapers. From our work, we're becoming more familiar with terms like "nonviolent resistance," "justice," and "oppression."

Mom comes to our next Jack and Jill meeting and helps Mrs. Dickerson lead a discussion on the use of nonviolence as a strategy for social change. I can tell that some of the Jack and Jill members don't believe King's nonviolence strategy will work. Others say it's working already.

I think Dr. King is right. I know that I'm now closely following the Birmingham campaign. By the third week, Dad shares with my brothers and me that campaign organizers are having trouble getting enough adults to continue the mass protests. The adults are afraid of losing their jobs or their lives. I wonder if the city ordinance and the letter from the White clergy have increased the fear level.

On Thursday, May 2, Dad has troubling news. There's been a change of strategy.

"A young associate of Dr. King's has trained students in junior high, high school, and college in the philosophy of nonviolence," Dad tells us. "Today, a thousand children participated in a massive protest march. The children walked out of their schools at noon and marched peacefully from the Sixteenth Street Baptist Church toward downtown Birmingham. The police arrested six hundred students before they reached town. It was a nonviolent march. I've been told that it will headline this evening's news. I came home from work early so that we can watch the report together."

I cover my mouth with my hands as if to silence a scream. "Did the children march by themselves?" I ask, shocked and excited by the news at the same time. I want to see that for myself.

"They did," Dad says.

"Jack, really . . . children?" Mom repeats.

"They're mostly teenagers, but it seems a few younger children marched, too," Dad explains. "Rachel, these children are already part of the movement. Some have attended meetings with their parents at the local churches and seen their moms and dads leave the house to protest, not knowing if they'll come back home for dinner or be sitting in a jail cell. All the children have lived with signs telling them that coloreds aren't welcome in stores and restaurants, and many other injustices. They've grown up only allowed to go to the fairgrounds on 'colored days.' The children of Birmingham are fed up and want their voices to be heard. I suspect that many will march with or without their parents' permission. They're fearless."

"I want to march," Jackie declares. "Can I go down, Dad?"

"To Birmingham?" Dad asks.

"Why not?" Jackie shoots back.

I hold my breath, waiting for Dad's response. If Dad says yes to Jackie, he might also agree to take me along.

"How about we march together . . . as a family . . . closer to home," Dad suggests.

I release a low sigh, not sure if I'm relieved or disappointed. "When?"

Jackie does not respond. He looks away from Dad. I know he's disappointed. David twists nervously in his chair and looks over at me. We're all shaken up by this turn of events. Children marching in the streets of Birmingham, wow. It must have been quite a sight.

We sit down together to watch the six o'clock news. I love this room with its shelves of books above the black leather couches and collection of encyclopedias at eye level. This is where my brothers and I come for information and a quiet place to read. The trouble is, these books don't contain current events. For that, we rely on newspaper stories and photographs, conversations with our parents and their community, and the nightly news. We have a nineteen-inch television set with ten channels and color picture in here as well. With this new television we are big time. Most of my friends only have black-and-white TVs.

David and I are lying on the carpet, waiting for the broadcast to begin. I'm resting on my elbows and looking up at Dad. I'm anxious to actually see the children. It amazes me that we're talking about kids going to jail because they're protesting against segregation. While we wait for the news, Mom checks in the almanac and lets us know that Birmingham, Alabama, is over one thousand miles from Stamford, Connecticut. That sounds like a long way to me, but Mom says we could be there in less than three hours if we flew from the airport in New York.

I hop up to get a glass of water as Dad turns on the television. After a greeting and quick summary of today's news, we see images of Black children walking down the middle of the street, singing songs. I stare into the faces of the children, thinking that many of them look like they are my age. Their faces look alive. Unafraid. They are laughing and singing, *"Ain't gonna let nobody turn me around. Turn me around. Turn me around."* I'm familiar with these words from other marches, but this is the first time I've heard them sung by children. I tear up and a shiver travels down my neck and shoulders.

Small bands of boys and girls are rounding up kids from other schools as they make their way toward the church. Thousands of students filing in the back door of the Sixteenth Street Baptist Church and coming out the church's front door in organized groups of fifty to one hundred.

"My God," Dad mutters.

I look up at my father, expecting him to say more about what we are seeing, but he just leans his elbows to his knees and stares silently at the screen. The pictures shift to children piling into police wagons and school buses.

"Are they going to jail?" I ask with tears spilling from my eyes.

"They are," Dad replies, leaning over to pat my shoulder. He is sitting on the couch between Mom and Grandma, his eyes glued to the television set.

"Look at that little boy," I scream, and point to the screen, horrified. "He looks younger than David."

"Jack, I thought they recruited college and high school students," Mom says as we watch the kids being stopped by police, arrested, and loaded into waiting vans and buses bound for jail.

"Shows you how quickly the word spread," Dad says. "Rachel, do you see the determination on the faces of those children?"

My mother is quiet.

I see it, too. The children hold their heads high and sing out loud and clear. Their feet pound the pavement in step to the music. Their picket signs read: SEGREGATION SOLD HERE and NO DIGNITY, NO DOLLARS. They look determined. A block and a half from the church, the police continue to lead them to waiting police wagons and school buses.

"The children were charged with parading without a permit," my dad says.

I watch in disbelief. Could this really be happening right here in America?

We hear that the police and firefighters were called to the scene, but there was no violence from either side. The report concludes by saying a thousand students marched and six hundred were arrested. It is the largest segregation protest demonstration in the history of the Deep South. And it was led by children.

As the news moves on to a different topic, our telephone rings. Dad grabs it on the second ring. He greets the caller, then grows silent, his facial expressions tightening and relaxing. Finally, he speaks. "You can count on me." I know this means that Dad is going into fund-raising mode. That night, he begins organizing an urgent meeting at Sardi's restaurant in the heart of New York City's theater district. Sardi's is a big gathering spot for politicians and celebrities. The walls are papered with silly caricatures of presidents and New York City mayors. Dad is hoping to gather a group of power hitters like the actor and singer Harry Belafonte.

On Friday night, my parents and I gather in the TV room to watch clips from the second day of the Children's March. Grandma's gone to the Covingtons' home in Brooklyn for the weekend. David's spending the night at the Calhouns. And Jackie is off playing pool with friends. Before we turn the television set on, Dad warns us. "I heard that Bull Connor called for the firemen to put the fire hoses on the children."

Dad's news is not a big surprise. Bull Connor is the commissioner of public safety for the city of Birmingham and a staunch segregationist. Dad had told us about some of the methods Bull Connor used in the city to stop protests, including the use of a big white tank that would show up to peaceful demonstrations, as well as the dogs and the fire hoses.

"Oh, Jack," Mom sobs. "I cannot believe that."

The first thing that comes to my mind is how in the summertime my brothers and I douse one another with water from the garden hose. We laugh and scream as the cold water hits our bare arms and legs. But Dad explains that the pressure from a fire hose can knock an adult off their feet, and I cradle my legs up to my chest as if to protect me from the pain. "Oh," I moan.

It's almost time to turn the news on, so I uncurl my body, get up, and walk over to the console to turn on the CBS evening news, then rush back to sit between Mom and Dad on the couch before we hear Walter Cronkite's voice. As the cameras flash to Birmingham, Cronkite warns us that we will see disturbing images as Bull Connor calls for violence against the peaceful young demonstrators.

For a second night in a row, we stare at the scene of children filing in and out of the Sixteenth Street Baptist Church. They wear sneakers and carry picket signs. A few kids wear raincoats because they had been warned about the fire hoses.

Cronkite sums up the day's march with flashes of video footage. I hold back tears as the police beat a boy with their batons. And I yell with fury when a police dog is sent chasing a group of frightened girls and boys. I wince as the camera shows Black boys and girls being knocked down by the force of water from the fire hoses. Their screams, as water bowls the children over and sends them cascading into one another, are too much. I sob uncontrollably.

"I dreamed last night that I was in Birmingham," I tell my parents after we've moved away from the news and are sharing a quiet meal at the kitchen table.

"Tell us about it," Mom urges.

"Well . . . in the dream, I was marching alongside a girl who was fourteen. She told me that her parents said not to march but she left school anyway. The girl is the oldest of five. She explained to me that she didn't want her younger brothers and sisters to think she's afraid to protest. She told me that it's right to fight for freedom. She wanted to be able to go to any school, sit in the movies, and walk into any store downtown. So she disobeyed her parents and showed up at the Sixteenth Street Baptist Church. We held arms. Both trembling. Surprisingly, the shaking stopped. I found myself smiling and singing along with the others. When I looked over at my new friend, I saw a glow around her face. It could have been the way the sun was hitting us, I don't know, but the girl looked so peaceful. It told me that she made the right decision and that her parents would someday agree."

"That's a beautiful dream," Mom says. "You've always been sensitive to children in trouble."

Dad nods in agreement. "Reminds me of the night Sharon heard what she thought was a baby crying. You woke us up saying someone's left us a baby," Dad says.

"You insisted that we come with you to open the front door," Mom adds.

"I was so disappointed," I tell them. "I'd heard that there were babies in orphanages waiting for good homes. I thought someone had dropped one of those babies off for us to adopt, but it was just a neighborhood cat."

"How does it make you feel to see children being put in the front lines of the movement?" asks Dad.

"I'm proud of the children and furious with the police," I say. "I thought attacking the kids with hoses and dogs was the worst part, but now I hate thinking of how frightened they must be in scary jail cells."

Later that evening, I overhear Dad unleash his own rage on a reporter calling about President Kennedy not getting involved in Birmingham. "Kennedy has the power to stop the violence against the children and to force civil rights legislation through Congress!" Dad shouts into the phone. Next I hear him say, "Of course, I'll go back to Birmingham! But not until we've raised enough money to get the children out of jail!"

"You tell him, Dad," I shout from the landing above the living room.

While Dad spends the next couple of days raising money and planning for the meeting at Sardi's, the children continue to protest in Birmingham, and American citizens press President Kennedy to stop the violence against the children.

At night, we all stop to watch the news and listen to the radio broadcasts. The tension in our living room is high. I'm finding it hard to bear, knowing the children are headed to jail. Tears fill my eyes when we hear that the Birmingham jails are filled and the state fairgrounds, the overflow site, is also almost full. A mother describes making sandwiches for the children in the fairgrounds and tossing the bags over the fence. Another sends her White employer to the fairgrounds to find out about her children. Another mother describes picking her daughter up from jail and learning that they'd been packed two to three hundred in a cell meant for fifty. We hear that a child as young as eight was in the march. During an interview with Reverend Fred Shuttlesworth, a reporter asks how much longer the demonstrations will go on, and he replies, "Until we run out of children."

There's praise for the courage of the children. There's also commentary in the newspapers weighing the pros and cons of sending children out into the front lines of the movement. Some Americans criticize the police for their use of fire hoses and dogs; others feel the battle should be waged in the courts. An activist named Malcolm X writes that he opposes the use of children in battle. President Kennedy avoids taking sides but makes it clear that his own concerns are for the safety of the children. He sends his brother Attorney General Robert F. Kennedy and a couple of his key civil rights aides, down to Birmingham.

The Children's Crusade continues to be on the front page of papers when the news breaks that the famous comedian Dick Gregory was arrested and jailed for four days for marching alongside the children.

My guilt about not being able to help is as bad as the constant worry. This week feels like it lasts a month. I think back to when Jackie ran away and how frightened we were. How terrified are the kids in Birmingham, unable to call home from jail? What does it feel like for their parents, not being able to see their children? I thought the police were around to protect us. Now I see them threatening children with their dogs. I see the force of water from fire hoses so great that children are rolling down the street. I see water push a girl over a car. Then I see children waving from a school bus as they're driven to jail.

I drag myself home from school the next day and find Dad waiting for me in the living room.

"The children have done it," Dad tells me.

I drop my books on the dining room table and step down into the living room. "What do you mean?"

"The protest marches have shut down the Birmingham businesses. Film actors, union leaders, and many others have flooded the White House with telegrams accusing the president of being indifferent to the racial issues in Birmingham. They told Kennedy that they were horrified by the images of children having their clothes torn off by dogs and them being tossed over cars by the force of water coming out of fire hoses. In the past, southern Blacks were beaten down by segregation. No more," Dad tells me.

I feel my shoulders fall and tears wet my eyes.

Dad puts his arms around me. "It's okay to cry, Sharon. Let it out. I know this has been a very stressful time, but we cannot let the stress break our spirits. That's why we saw the children laughing and singing as they were transported to jail. They've lived with fear all their lives. Now they know that they can fight back against segregation and be heard. That's what's most important here. Sure, it's just a first step. But it's a step forward. Their actions have given all of us courage. We cannot sit back and accept injustice. We have to say, 'enough.' I'm an American citizen. A human being. I'm willing to go to jail for freedom. Cry at night. Wake up with joy. Greet the new day with faith and determination. Does that make sense?"

I sit up straight and wipe my eyes. "Sounds like what you'd say when we'd fall off our bikes. That we need to get back up," I say, smiling through my tears. "I'm proud of the kids in Birmingham, Dad. Not sure I'd have that much courage."

"Oh, I don't know about that," Dad replies. "Not many kids would ride a horse bareback or confront their principal, demanding to be moved up to a new class so they could take a foreign language. You're strong and determined, Sharon. I bet if you lived in Birmingham, you would have insisted on marching."

"I wanted to go to Birmingham, Dad. Just not to jail," I admit.

"No one wants to go to jail, sweetheart."

"Dad, will they release all the children now?"

Dad's face clouds over. "Many are still in jail, and most will go to court to defend their actions," he tells me. "City officials are trying to suspend the children who marched from school. It's another battle. Lawyers from the NAACP will get involved. There is plenty of work to do."

"How can I get involved?"

"Right now, your responsibility is to get the best education you can. That is one way you can ensure you have future options. This battle to end racism will be as important when you're an adult as it is now. We'll need lawyers, doctors, nurses, accountants, and firemen to keep our community healthy and strong," Dad reminds me.

I glance up at him, not sure that was the right answer. "What about protest marches?"

"We'll do that, too, someday," he says, then adds, "as a family."

I'm relieved that Dad really hears my need to be more involved. I hear him, too. "If I want joy in the morning, I better get my homework done," I say, leaning over to kiss Dad's cheek.

CHAPTER 21

I'm so happy that my social studies paper on Dr. King's letter from a Birmingham jail has spurred debate at Dolan. My homeroom teacher, Mrs. Chipouras, calls me up to her desk before the first bell.

"I read your paper on Dr. King," she says, speaking softly.

I'm shocked. I'd written that paper for social studies, so how did Mrs. Chipouras get ahold of it? I am about to ask, when she speaks up again.

"You did a good job," Mrs. Chipouras says. "It convinced me to pay more attention to what's been going on in Birmingham."

It feels good to have my work praised. "I didn't know teachers shared their students' papers with other teachers."

"Only when one stands out," she replies. "We were in the teacher's lounge having lunch, and the Children's March in Birmingham came up. Your social studies teacher mentioned your paper and shared it with me later. That was a week ago. I made a point of studying the issues." Mrs. Chipouras paused. "I want to hold a debate and get the students here thinking about the civil rights movement. What do you think?"

I hold my breath, then release it slowly. I honestly don't think my classmates are ready to talk about race. I'm not even sure I could do it in front of them. It wouldn't be like Jack and Jill, where everyone in the room is Black. This would be a single Black girl speaking in a room full of White kids about racial injustice. No, I don't think it's a good idea. "I don't know if kids have enough information for a debate," I reply.

"Interesting," she says, fidgeting with a pen and following me with her eyes. "You might be right, but it's being discussed at our school board meetings right here in Stamford."

"I know," I say without giving an opinion.

"Okay. Thanks for your perspective," Mrs. Chipouras tells me as the bell rings and I hustle to my seat with a dozen pairs of eyes following me.

After the Pledge of Allegiance and morning notes, Mrs. Chipouras stands in front of the class to discuss current events. "How many of you have seen television footage of children leading a protest march in Birmingham, Alabama?"

I lift my hand without removing my gaze from Mrs. Chipouras's face. She gives my classmates a description of the march. "I watched the news captivated by the courage of those young people and horrified by the reaction of the police. The children were peaceful even when under direct attack by the force of water shooting from fire hoses or a policeman urging his German shepherd toward them. The marchers are demanding freedom. Can anyone tell me what freedom they're fighting for?"

I bolt upright and look to my right and left. My White classmates are stone-faced. I wonder if they don't understand the question or if they're afraid to speak up. I raise my hand.

Mrs. Chipouras nods toward me.

"They're marching to gain freedom from segregation and racial injustice," I say, then pause. "There is civil rights legislation that needs to be voted on by the House of Representatives and then signed by President Kennedy. If passed, discrimination based on race, color, religion, sex, or national origin will be outlawed and constitutional rights will be granted to all Americans."

"Thank you, Sharon." Mrs. Chipouras turns to the rest of the room. "As your classmate explained, passage of the Civil Rights Act would enforce the constitutional right to vote and equal opportunity in education and employment for all Americans. As always, I reserve a few minutes in the morning to discuss current events, hoping to motivate you to know what's going on in the world around you. This issue affects us all. Please don't think it's just a problem for Birmingham, Alabama."

"My mom says that Stamford is starting a busing program because the public schools are segregated," one of the students points out.

Mrs. Chipouras smiles. "That's correct, Peter."

"I wanted to go to Rippowam, but looks like we'll be bused downtown to Stamford High," Peter adds.

"Stamford High is a great school," Mrs. Chipouras reminds us.

Behind me, I hear students shifting in their seats and whispering. I'm looking at my homeroom teacher with new admiration. She is brave to bring up this touchy subject and to point out that the problems are not just in the Deep South.

"I understand that talking about race can be uncomfortable for many people, but we're in the middle of change right here in our own community. I read Sharon Robinson's social studies paper and was inspired to pay attention to the crisis in Birmingham. The children in Birmingham have set the bar high. They're lifting their voices and becoming leaders in the movement to end segregation in America. I hope you'll pay attention and feel inspired. That's all for this morning, class," Mrs. Chipouras tells us as the bell rings.

I file out of class flanked by classmates asking me questions about the Children's March.

"What is it?"

"Could it happen in Stamford?"

"Did they really arrest children and put them in jail?"

A girl even asks me if I'd gone down to Birmingham to join the march. I speak quickly, hitting points I've heard from my mom and dad at home. It amazes me that my paper really stirred up this new interest in segregation.

I enter my language arts class wondering if the students who spoke to me really understand the sacrifice we'll all have to make to break down segregation in our community.

I settle into my seat. I realize that the children in Birmingham have opened my eyes to the importance of the civil rights movement. Mrs. Chipouras gave us all a challenge this morning and I want to find a way to keep the discussion going instead of shying away from talking about race and segregation with my White friends. From now on, I will push myself to stand up for what I believe.

I can't wait to get home and tell Dad about my morning. I now have a greater appreciation for what he's been trying to do in taking on this fight for equality.

This is why I admire my father. He uses his celebrity to push for change. I'm anxious about his next trip to Birmingham. But it's important that he shows his support in person.

I've learned that every day, there is a new crisis. As Dad is preparing to fly to Birmingham, we learn that the A. G. Gaston

Motel has been bombed. This is the only Negro-owned motel in Birmingham. Dr. King and his group are staying there. He's safe, but three other people are injured. I wonder if the news will change Dad's plans, but the next day, he and heavyweight champion boxer Floyd Patterson fly to Birmingham for a rally with Dr. King, Ralph Abernathy, and Wyatt Tee Walker at the Fifth Baptist Church.

I can barely concentrate at school. I'm so worried. I've never traveled to the Deep South, so my only images of cities like Birmingham are what we read in newspapers and see on the news. If those clergymen in Birmingham called Dr. King an outsider, people may think Dad and Floyd Patterson are going there to stir up trouble. That terrifies me. If Dad's arrested, how will he get his insulin shots? My mind flips between worry and pride. I know that my father is doing what's right.

Dad calls minutes before we sit down to dinner. I rush to the phone just to hear his voice. I listen quietly as he tells Mom that he and Floyd look like the walking wounded with his cane and Floyd's bandaged hand, an injury from his last boxing match. He's laughing as he talks. His voice drops as he describes a packed church and thunderous applause when he and Floyd walked down the center aisle. Dad tells Mom that they're staying at the A. G. Gaston Motel with Dr. King and the others. Mom's hesitation reminds me that he'll be staying at the same hotel that was just bombed. I choke up. Covering the mouthpiece, I clear my throat and manage to speak before Dad hangs up, "Dad," I say into the phone, afraid he'll be gone before I can tell him anything.

"How's my sweetheart?" he asks.

"I'm scared," I admit.

"Floyd and I are surrounded by people at all times. There's no need to worry," he tells me.

"What about your knee?"

"It's holding up just fine. I'll see you tomorrow night."

"Mom says you're coming home late and that it's a school night," I complain.

"I'll ask her to let you stay up until I get home. It won't be too late."

"Love you, Dad," I whisper.

"Love you so much," he replies.

I hang up the phone in the kitchen and run back to the dining room. "Aren't you scared?" I ask my mother.

She nods. "Your father wouldn't let fear keep him from going down to Birmingham. He and Floyd Patterson are loved. They will be safe," Mom assures me.

Grandma wraps an arm around me. "Help me get dinner on the table. Okay?"

I lean into my grandmother and fight back tears. "Okay," I tell her.

Later, I lie in bed, staring at the flowers on my canopy, feeling safe, free, and guilty. I have so much compared to the children in Birmingham. I wonder when they'll get to have some of the freedoms I take for granted. Simple things like going to the movie theater and ordering milkshakes at the downtown diner. I feel my eyes getting heavy and giving in to sleep. One last thought crosses my mind. When the protest marches end, what happens next? Do the children get out of jail and go back to school? They've lived with segregation, bombings, and threats to their lives. They've seen their parents march for freedom. Now they've marched and gone to jail themselves. How will they continue to be involved in the civil rights movement? How will their sacrifice be remembered? Now that they have found a way to express their anger and frustration with segregation, what is the next step for them and me? I close my eyes and settle my head on my pillow.

The next night, Mom and I wait up for Dad. The house is quiet with David, Willette, and Grandma asleep and Jackie out with his friends. Dad called earlier to say they'd arrived back from Birmingham and that he'll be home after he attends a voter-registration rally in the city.

There's a slight chill in the living room, so Mom and I decide to make a fire. I pile in the kindling and logs. Mom stuffs newspaper around the logs and uses matches to light it. We settle on the couch and stare as flames shoot up the chimney.

I'm excited for Dad to walk in so he can tell us all about his trip.

"Mrs. Chipouras told me that she read my social studies paper on Dr. King's letter from a Birmingham jail. It made her pay attention to the news reports. She wanted to share my paper with our class, but I didn't want her to," I tell Mom.

"It was a good paper, Sharon. You should be proud of it," Mom says.

"Too embarrassing," I say. "Instead, she talked about the Children's March in our current events time. I think the kids were really interested in Birmingham. One of the boys brought up Stamford's school desegregation plan. That got everyone's attention."

"That's incredible," Mom says when I'm done talking about my classmates' reactions to the discussion. "You and Mrs. Chipouras linked your classmates to Birmingham and to the realities of the struggle to end segregation. I'm so proud of you, Sharon," Mom says, checking her watch. "Your father—"

"Is home," I interrupt at the sound of the garage door opening.

I follow Mom to the top of the stairs. "Dad," I call out as he comes through the door on the lower level.

"Where are the boys?" Dad asks after hugging Mom and me.

"David's asleep. Jackie's out but should be home soon."

Dad looks at his watch and frowns.

I grab Dad's hand and pull him toward the living room. "We lit a fire."

"In May . . ." He chuckles. "Sure feels good." He kisses me on the forehead.

"Tell us about Birmingham," Mom says after he's settled on the sofa between us.

"Did you meet any of the kids?" I ask.

"I did," Dad said. "They asked about you kids. I told them that all three of you have been following their story and that we as a family were very proud of them."

I beam.

"All things considered, it was a good trip. The mood was upbeat even with the most recent bombing. The Birmingham business community has agreed to work with the Black community to strip away segregation. Everyone understands that this is just a first step with a lot of work to come," Dad explains. "But folks put away their worries for one night and celebrated. Dr. King held an enormous rally at the church. The place was packed. The music lifted all our spirits. They treated Floyd and me like royalty. Dr. King praised the children and said their courage and strength captured the attention of the world and will be a tremendous help with the passage of the Civil Rights Act.

"When people saw Floyd's bandaged hand, they asked him if he could still beat Sonny Liston and win back the title. Floyd had the ladies roaring with laughter. After the rally, we went to a reception. A young boy asked if I wanted to see his leg. He pulled up his pants. His shin was covered in a bandage where a police dog had bitten him. He said the tetanus shot hurt almost as much as the bite. Strong little guy."

I wince at the dog bite and the shot.

"I met a well-known radio announcer named Shelley Stewart. He sent signals during his show to the young marchers that it was time to march. Several of the local DJs did the same thing. Of course, he couldn't say things outright. So he came up with clever phrases."

"Did he tell you any of them?" I ask, giggling.

"'It's time to shake, rattle, and roll' meant it was time to march. When Shelley announced that 'it's going to rain today,' he meant they planned on using fire hoses against the marchers."

I'm laughing so hard, I fall off the sofa. Jumping up, Mom signals for me to settle down. "He sounds like a cool guy," I say.

"Shelley's young . . . not much older than some of the marchers. His nickname is 'The Playboy.' The kids listen to him. He even tells them to bring their toothbrushes in case they have to spend the night in jail."

"He sounds like quite a character," Mom says. "Jack, did you meet any parents who refused to let their children march?"

"I heard the story of a mother who was booed for dragging her son off the line. Then I met Dale." Dad pauses. "Apparently, we'd met before when I spoke at the Sixteenth Street Baptist Church. Dale said he was too young to understand the significance of 'meeting Jackie Robinson' back then. He remembers being pushed onstage by his mother when I was there. Dale and his younger brother are good friends with Dr. King's nephews. They'd been in on the plans for the Children's March, but their parents wouldn't let Dale and his brother march. I could tell that Dale felt like he'd let his friends down."

Listening to Dad talk, I try to imagine who I'd be if we lived in a place like Birmingham. Would I be an activist who defied my mother if she told me I couldn't march?

"Was his mom worried he'd go to jail?" I ask.

"I think she was also afraid of losing her job," Dad replies.

"That was probably a real threat," Mom says.

"Dale's a smart boy. He obeyed his parents but told them they couldn't protect him from racism," Dad says.

"He's right. Isn't he, Dad?"

"Told you he's a smart boy."

"He also has a smart mother who is trying to protect him. You look tired, Jack. We should all go to bed and finish this conversation tomorrow," Mom suggests.

"Just one more story . . . please, Daddy," I beg.

"One more," Dad says. "I was introduced to this woman named Marie Montgomery. She's a passionate activist. Marie brought all five of her kids to planning meetings for the Birmingham campaign. Each week they went to a different location to keep the meetings secret.

"The whole family marched, even her youngest daughter, Janice. She let the older children, Carolyn and James, march in the Children's Crusade. Carolyn spent over a week in jail. James was held at the fairgrounds. Marie said that the children suffered in the overcrowded jails. She prays that she did the right thing by letting them march. Marie told me that families have lived their entire lives afraid for themselves and their children. They've had enough."

"Dad, is it all over now?" I ask.

Dad turns to me, looking very tired. "It pains me to say this, but the struggle for racial justice will probably go on all our lives. We can change the laws, but it's harder to change behavior and attitudes. We may live in the North, but racism is here, too. It shows up in different ways. That's why we push you and your brothers to do your best in school. That's your job now.

Later, if you're prepared, you will have work that you love and the ability to make a life filled with purpose."

I stand up and hug my parents. "I love hearing the stories, Dad, but I feel sad, too," I tell him. I want a happy ending.

"I want to talk more about this with the whole family. There's still more to do," Dad says as I head to bed.

CHAPTER 22

The next night, we are all around the dinner table with plates of hot food in front of us. But instead of eating, we're listening to David's saga from the final minutes of his lacrosse game. He waves his hands and moves his feet to make us understand the urgency of the elite private-school sport. Personally, I'm ready to dive into my mashed potatoes and hear Dad's news, but it's the fourth quarter in a tense game. We have to let David finish.

"I jumped in and scooped the ball up into my stick." David swings his arms forward as he speaks. "The goalie didn't have a chance. The ball flew across the goal line and gave us the winning point."

We all clap and cheer David's team's victory. Dad blesses the table and my fork heads straight for the pool of gravy in the middle of the mashed potatoes. It's baked chicken night, and we're all starving.

"What's new on your end, Jackie?"

"Not much," he says. "Trying to pass algebra."

"You've always been good at math," Dad comments.

"That's changed," Jackie says.

"Do you need help?" Mom offers. "We could look into a tutor."

"This girl at school's helping me," he says.

"Oh, who is that?"

"Just some girl who sits next to me."

"Dad, you said we could talk about Birmingham," I say.

"That's all you want to talk about," David moans.

"We'll get to it," Dad tells me.

We chat until the plates are cleared from the table. Then all eyes turn to Dad.

"Your mother and I have come up with a way for the entire family to help raise money for Birmingham."

Really? I'm excited that they want us to be more involved.

"Do you know what 'legacy' means?" Dad asks.

I look to my brothers. I have no idea and from the look on David's and Jackie's faces, they don't either.

"I've heard of it," Jackie says. "It's an inheritance, right?"

"That's one definition, son. But it can mean more than the passing along of money or property. We want to build a

Robinson family legacy and pass along a belief in a cause and the desire to serve others," Dad explains.

I'm still confused. How do you do that?

"Here's the way it goes," Dad says as if reading my thoughts. "By breaking the color barrier in baseball, I helped open the doors for other players to follow. Sixteen years later, baseball teams all have Black players on their rosters. It did another thing as well. Because we were successful in baseball, it gave others hope and inspiration to fight to end segregation in all areas of American life. Responsibility comes along with that success and it funnels down to you kids as well. People look to us to help force change and racial justice. That is our legacy."

"But how do we do that without going down to the South?" I ask.

"Good question, Sharon. Rae, do you want to share our plan with the children?"

"Raising money is one of the important ways families in the North can support the desegregation efforts in the South," Mom began. "For years, your father has been traveling throughout the country, raising money so lawyers can fight in the courts and protesters can be bailed out of jail. Well, we've found a way to involve the entire family in our fund-raising efforts. We're planning to hold a jazz concert right here," Mom explains. "The six acres of our property, the sloping back lawn, will be a perfect music venue. Our first concert will be held on

Sunday, June twenty-third. The show will be a fund-raiser for Dr. King and the Southern Christian Leadership Conference. Your father and I are working with our friends Marian and Arthur Logan to ask some famous jazz artists to volunteer to perform at the concert."

I stare at Mom, surprised by how quickly they've come up with this plan. A jazz concert on our lawn. I love the idea!

"You may not realize this, but Marian Logan is a jazz singer. She knows many of the artists. And her husband, Dr. Arthur Logan, is Duke Ellington's personal physician. We've all been reaching out to the musicians and so far the response has been terrific. They're anxious to help raise money for the movement. The best part is that they're willing to perform without charging a fee," Mom says.

"Concerts are expensive so we're asking everyone to volunteer and help us. Some people will sell tickets while others will set up the stage and help with the artists. Your grandmother has offered to bake some of her delicious cakes, and we'll raffle them off."

"What can we do?" I ask.

"Jackie, I'd like you to join me at the entrance to the driveway. We'll greet our guests and tell them where to park. How does that sound?" Dad says.

"Good," Jackie says.

"What about me?" David pipes up.

Mom touches his hand. "We'd like for you and Sharon to sell sodas, water, and hot dogs. It's a big job. The stand will be staffed by children. We've begun making a list of kids. You can ask your friends to help out. It will be a long, hot day, so we'll need at least twenty children to cover all the shifts throughout the event," Mom explains.

"The goal will be to get everything we can donated. So most of the money we'll raise from ticket sales will go to Birmingham," Dad says.

"Even the hot dogs?" David asks.

"Hot dogs. Sodas. Napkins. Paper plates. You name it . . . we'll find a way to get it donated," Mom tells us.

"This is amazing!" I say. "I know Candy and her family will help, and I think Christy would, too."

"Michael and a few kids at my school will also help out," David chips in.

"Mrs. Dickerson is making a list of children from your Jack and Jill chapter. We will be having lots of guests and performers in the house," Mom tells us. "You'll have to get up very early in the morning and clean your rooms so the performers will have a place to change clothes. That includes your closet, Sharon . . ."

I grin sheepishly. My closet is always a mess. "I'll start working on it this weekend," I promise.

"We expect that it will be a big event with hundreds of guests and probably a dozen performers. Are you excited?" Dad asks.

"Very," I say.

"Me, too, but what does this have to do with legacy?" David asks.

"We'll be giving back to others as a family. If we're successful, there will be more concerts and other ways for us to work together toward change. That, son, is our legacy."

"We'll sell a million cans of soda!" David shouts.

"And two hundred thousand hot dogs," I add.

"Will Martin Luther King be here?" Jackie wants to know.

I'm blown away. Martin Luther King may be coming to our house?

"His schedule is unpredictable, son. He knows of our plans and will be here if he can," Dad says.

"I really want to meet him," Jackie says.

"So do I," David and I both chime in at the same time.

"I will work very hard to make that happen," Dad promises.

CHAPTER 23

For the next few weeks, we're consumed with the upcoming jazz concert. The Logans own and live in a five-story brownstone building on the Upper West Side of Manhattan. Their fund-raising parties for political candidates and civil rights organizations are famous. Mom and Dad go to the Logans' house for jazz concert meetings, and they host meetings in our living room, too.

I love the energy that the concert planning has brought to our home. I love that I'm actually involved, not just watching other kids do something on the news. We celebrate every ticket sale and donation we receive. The list of jazz artists expected to perform grows every day. My brothers and I don't know most of the names, so Mom plays their records to get us familiar with the music. It adds to the excitement.

As the day approaches, our garages fill with cases of soda,

hot dogs, ketchup, relish, mustard, and cans of beer. David and I race around the yard telling everyone we encounter how many crates have arrived. Extra refrigerators are added throughout the lower level of our home. We count how many packages of hot dogs they'll hold. Plastic forks, spoons, and knives are delivered a week before the big event.

Menus are prepared. The plan is to provide home-cooked meals for the artists. The living room rug is shampooed. Dad cuts the lawns. We prune the gardens.

Mom fills the house with jazz. The sounds of jazz trumpeter Dizzy Gillespie, and Ella Fitzgerald putting her Grammy-winning voice to a jazzy version of the nursery rhyme "A-Tisket A-Tasket" blast from the record player. My brothers and I quickly get into the beats and hum along to the tunes. I can barely contain my excitement.

We find out a week before the concert that Dr. King will not be able to attend. We're disappointed, but we're so busy that it doesn't slow us down.

Days before, Mom and I go to the nursery for colorful plants to fill the planters on the patio. Afterward, Mrs. Dickerson, who's in charge of the children-run concession stands, gathers us together to talk about selling sodas and hot dogs. Twenty children have volunteered to work the concert. Mrs. Dickerson walks us through a sales pitch, then pairs up the kids so we can practice.

"Hi, my name's Sharon. Every soda you purchase today goes directly to SCLC. How many sodas would you like?" I ask Kimberly, Candy's younger sister.

"I'll take two," Kimberly replies. "What's the name of that organization?"

"SCLC stands for Southern Christian Leadership Conference. It's Dr. Martin Luther King's organization," I reply, pretending to hand Kimberly two sodas. "Did you see the Children's March last month on the news?"

"You mean the horrible pictures of the police spraying children with fire hoses?"

"That's right. Well, money raised at this concert will help pay the children's bail money and support Dr. King's work. Sure you don't want to add a couple of hot dogs?" I ask, using all the techniques I learned, in hope of upping the sale.

"I'll take two hot dogs and another orange soda." Kimberly pretends to hand me five dollars.

"Thank you for your support! I hope you enjoy the concert," I say, putting the money into the metal box.

Mrs. Dickerson claps her hands. "Good job!" she tells us.

Kimberly and I join the others for a wrap-up that includes the importance of us staying hydrated, counting the money, and taking breaks.

We regularly check the weather reports. Rain is our big concern and the one factor we can't control. Mom knows what to do. She turns her head to the sky and says, "Please, Lord."

Our prayers are answered. Sunday, June 23, the house, gardens, and grass look beautiful!

David pounces on my bed at six fifteen. "Get up, sis!"

I peek from under my covers. "Is it morning already?" I ask, yawning and opening my eyes for the first time.

"Mom said to get up and make sure your bedroom is spotless," David tells me. "She's inspecting our rooms at six forty-five."

"Is your room ready?"

"It will be," David replies, peeking over at my closet. "I see clothes on your closet floor. You're going to be in trouble."

"Get off my bed," I scold, pushing his back. "Worry about your own mess. I'll be done way before you." I hop out of bed and race to the bathroom to shower and brush my teeth.

At six forty-five, I'm dressed in blue shorts and a T-shirt, greeting the folks who have arrived early to cook. The kitchen smells of frying chicken and cakes baking in the oven. Grandma is in charge, directing the making of potato and green salads while she whips up chocolate frosting.

I attempt to stick my finger in the bowl, but Grandma swats it away with a wooden spoon. "Don't you dare, young lady. Make yourself a bowl of cold cereal so you and David can get to work. Your father and Jackie are already gone to map out the parking lots."

"On it," I tell my grandmother, and make a second attempt to sneak a taste of the frosting.

"Sharon!" Grandma scolds.

I walk away giggling.

David and I drag folding tables down to the section of the lawn reserved for selling drinks and hot dogs. The stage is set up with a green-and-white striped canopy covering the raised wooden structure.

I spot vans coming onto the grassy area and shout to David, "Look out for the vans!" We stop piling warm soda cans into metal buckets of ice long enough to watch the men unload gigantic speakers. Across the lawn, a group of volunteers is laying out stacks of AFTERNOON OF JAZZ T-shirts. We're all busy and having fun at the same time. By the time our buckets are filled with cans of soda, music is piping through the speakers and folks are dancing to the beats. We're ready!

At ten, Dad and Jackie open the gates and greet guests as they drive onto the grounds. The artists arrive in limos and are escorted into our home to relax and refresh before heading down to the stage to perform.

We sell over six hundred tickets to the concert, with each guest paying a donation of ten dollars or more. It's a great time, with picnic lunches, warm sunshine, baskets, and blankets, everyone enjoying a wonderful concert on the lawn. A few neighbors row their boats down the lake and enjoy the seven-hour concert from there.

Everyone brags about the day, including eighty tired but happy volunteers. David and I are thrilled to report to Mom and Dad that the sale of sodas and hot dogs raised a whopping $1,100! Dizzy Gillespie, Dave Brubeck, and the Cannonball Adderley Quintet are a few of the acts that perform.

At the conclusion of the concert, I stand out front with my parents thanking our guests for coming and supporting civil rights. We hear over and over that it was a great day. The best news is we raised a total of $15,000! That will go a long way toward the cause.

We stay outside with large black bags, picking up trash until it is too dark to see and we are too tired to stand upright. Inside the house, friends are still washing dishes, vacuuming carpets, and rehashing a wonderful day.

My brothers and I flop onto the couch, laughing and sharing stories. Mom and Dad join us after the last of the volunteers leave. We talk until our minds and bodies are limp and it's a physical challenge to walk down the hall to our rooms.

When Dad and Mom first talked about a family mission, I couldn't conceive of anything so amazing as the Afternoon of Jazz. I climb into bed and fill my diary with notes from this amazing experience. It has introduced a new world to me. I can't wait to find out how else we can build our family's legacy.

CHAPTER 24

"Chock full o'Nuts is sponsoring a sleepover camp for the children of employees," Dad announces over pancakes. "I signed you and David up."

I'm not sure how I feel about this new camp. I've only ever been to Girl Scout sleepover camps. I figure this one will be different, but I need more information.

"You mean boys and girls will be at the same camp? But wait, Dad . . . if it's for employees, won't most of the kids be Black?" I have more questions, but these are the first that come to mind.

"Will there be fishing?" David asks.

"I guess I threw that one on you too quickly," Dad says. "The camp will be in upstate New York. It's a beautiful site with a nice lake. You can swim, boat, and fish in it. The boys will be in one dormitory and the girls in another. And yes, most of the campers will be Black."

"Wow!" This will be like Jack and Jill kids going to a sleepover camp. This was turning out to be a summer of firsts. My first Jack and Jill dance, the jazz concert, and now a camp with other Black kids. The shift is almost too much to comprehend. The mostly White environment of my childhood is quickly giving way as I'm exposed more to the Black world.

"Can Candy come?" I ask, figuring she and I can enjoy this cultural shift together.

"Sure," Dad replies. "Your cousins JoJo, Kirk, and Chuckie are going as well."

"Yay," I say, though my heart is slamming against my chest. "How long is camp?"

"Two weeks," Mom says.

"When do we go?" David asks with little enthusiasm.

"Right after the Fourth of July," Dad says.

I have mixed feelings. I definitely want to go to this new camp, but I also love unstructured summer days at our home in Stamford. Diamond and I have plenty of time to explore and bond. I can spend time volunteering at the nature center nearby and taking care of a variety of animals. And Christy and I always use the time to create a new water ballet in her pool.

I'm excited to jump into this new territory. I imagine a camp of Black kids listening to Motown records, learning the latest dances from kids who live in Brooklyn, Queens, and the Bronx, and making new friends. Pretty cool except I remember we're leaving something important behind.

"Who will take care of Diamond while David and I are away at camp?" I ask my parents.

"We've got him covered," Mom says. "Your former horse trainer is going to board him while you're away. You and David have done a great job keeping up with him and your schoolwork. It will be nice to have a two-week break."

"I could stay home," David offers.

"No, we want you both to have this experience. The camp is your father's idea. It's important that we give it full family support. You'll make new friends and have fun."

"What about Jackie?" I ask.

"He doesn't want to go to camp. Most of the children will be younger than Jackie. Your father and I will bring him with us into the city for a couple of days," Mom explains.

"What about our trip to Montauk?" David wants to know.

"The whole family will spend July Fourth weekend in Montauk so we can fish and enjoy time at the beach as usual."

"Yay!" David screams out.

I love going to Montauk, too, but not to fish. Dad, Jackie, and David will fish from the shores while Mom and I walk the beach, looking for driftwood. Montauk is pretty isolated, and there are no golf courses to pull Dad away from the family. Dad usually rents a fishing boat with a captain who takes us out to the deep Atlantic Ocean to fish. We all get seasick but recover enough in time to enjoy fishing from the boat. In fact, that's the only way I enjoy fishing.

"Yuck!" I say, remembering hanging my head over the boat ledge to vomit into the ocean. "Maybe this year we won't all get seasick," I suggest.

"This year you'll take a pill to control that," Mom tells me.

"That's good," I say, perking up.

"I can't wait! I'll win the biggest fish contest again this year," David says as Jackie strolls into the kitchen.

"Last year was the first time your fish was bigger than mine," Jackie reminds David. "I intend to take back the title."

"Wanna bet?" David challenges.

"You're on," Jackie says as he forks a stack of pancakes onto his plate.

Dad chuckles at the banter between the boys.

"If I win, you come with Sharon and me to Chock full Camp," David suggests.

Jackie looks up at David like he's crazy. His mouth is full of pancakes, but there's no mistaking the direction of his head shake.

* * *

A week later, we drive through Long Island to Montauk, a small fishing village along the coast. We all like the fact that it's so far away from our busy life. Our days are filled with fishing, swimming, and walking the beach. At night, the boys set up the grill for hot dogs, hamburgers, and our catch of the day. I love seeing Mom and Dad so happy and relaxed.

After a long weekend, we drive back to Connecticut and pack for camp. I call Candy every hour.

"Are you packing a dress?"

"For camp?"

"Sure. Suppose there's a dance. Or a cute boy," I reply.

"You've got a point," Candy replies.

I add two sundresses to my luggage and one pair of cute sandals. Then call Candy back.

"You know the campers mostly live in New York?"

"I figured that," Candy replies.

"Imagine they'll teach us some new dances, right?" I suggest.

"Sure," Candy says. "We'll have some new moves to show off at the next dance."

I hang up, picturing myself sitting next to a nice boy at dinner and maybe holding hands as we walk around the campsite. Candy is already fourteen. I have to wait for January, again, but we're both excited to be entering ninth grade in September. Boys have been the hot topic since seventh grade. Now that we're upperclassmen at Dolan, we're hoping to really have some experiences to talk about.

I'm still grinning over the prospect of a boyfriend when we pick up Candy at her house the next day. The back seat of Dad's Cadillac is roomy enough. I sit in the middle to give Candy's legs more space. David, I notice, is clinging to the left side of the car and not looking too happy. Mom and Dad chat in the front seat. When we stop for gas, David maneuvers his way into the front seat to escape our whispers. Candy and I stretch out in the back seat and escape into our books.

When we arrive, the three of us run around to check out the campgrounds. Pleased with our findings, we meet up with Mom and Dad for the orientation. Our cousins have arrived as well. Kirk cries when his parents leave. His twin sister scolds him gently until he stops crying. At the first meal, Chuckie, who is the oldest but who also hates most foods, refuses to eat. I have little hope that they'll survive even the first week. Sure enough, Uncle Chuck picks up his children on the third day of camp. I'm sad to see Jojo leave. She is two years younger than me but always good for a laugh. Candy, David, and I adjust to camp life and have fun with the daily activities. We love being around so many other Black kids.

By the fourth day, I notice this boy. He's playing basketball with a bunch of kids and keeps looking my way. He's taller than most of the other kids and thin with curly black hair cut close to his scalp. I watch closely as he makes a layup. Candy and I are sitting on a bench outside the basketball court.

I realize that I'm staring at the boy with the friendly smile and he's glancing back at me. I lean over and point him out to Candy. "He's cute," she admits.

The boy bends over to catch his breath. His hands rest on his knees. As he straightens up, he notices me pointing at him and smiles. I smile back, then look away quickly.

The boys' game winds down and the girls walk onto the court. As I pass the cute boy, he speaks. "Good luck."

I look up and return his smile. "Thanks," I say.

The girls are only allowed to play half-court basketball. It is really silly. Do they think girls can't run up and down a full court without fainting from exhaustion? The setup frustrates me, especially in front of this new boy. Still, I'm good at basketball. After one really good block, I look up and see that the boy is watching me. I look away and try to stay focused on the game, but he stays in my head. *Will I see him at dinner?*

That night, I spot the boy on line all the way across the dining room from my table. He's looking in my direction. I put my camp bag on the seat next to me just in case. Candy is sitting opposite me. She laughs at my not-so-subtle move.

"Is this seat taken?" the boy asks. His voice is deep.

I look up while smiling at him and snatch my bag off the chair.

"My name's Randy," he says, settling down next to me.

"I'm Sharon," I say, and point to Candy. "That's my best friend, Candy."

Randy reaches across the table to shake Candy's hand, which impresses me. *He's got manners*, I think. He's also even cuter close up. We eat and chat about camp.

Our days and evenings are so structured. In the mornings, we're taken on nature hikes through the woods, where the counselors teach us about different types of birds, plants, trees, and wildflowers. Art classes are also held in the morning. After lunch, we have water activities. I usually see David at the lake swimming, rowboating, canoeing, and fishing—all the things he enjoys at home. We're grouped according to our swimming ability. Everyone takes an hour swimming lesson each day. My advanced swimming group also likes to show off our diving skills.

"You're a good swimmer," Randy tells me.

"How do you know?" I ask.

"Been checking you out," he admits.

I feel my face get hot. "It's my favorite sport," I manage to say. "You obviously play a lot of basketball."

"I'm on the high school team," he tells me. "I like the gap between your front teeth," Randy adds.

I take a big gulp of lemonade and almost have to spit it back out. *That's so personal*, I think, and then realize it's also the first time anyone's complimented me on the gap between my front teeth. "I wish it wasn't there."

"Where I come from, it's a sign of beauty," Randy explains.

Beauty! I glance up at Candy. She's stifling a giggle. *That's crazy*, I think, yet Randy's comment makes me happy. *Does he think I'm pretty?* I push my tray forward, too flustered to finish the meat loaf and corn, and shift the subject away from me. "How old are you?" I ask.

"Fourteen," he replies. "But I turn fifteen in October. What about you?"

"Oh, I'm thirteen and a half," I reply, hoping he won't think I'm too young.

Randy looks over at Candy. "I'm fourteen, too," she tells him.

"Where are you girls from?" Randy asks.

"Stamford, Connecticut," Candy says. "It's an hour from New York City."

"Where do you live?" I ask, feeling more comfortable with this line of questions.

"I live in the Bronx and pretty much stay where there's public transportation. You've probably never ridden in the subway," Randy suggests.

"No such thing in Connecticut," I say, thinking how different our lives must be. "It's all long walks to the bus stops out in the country, but I come into the city with my dad sometimes. He drives in from Connecticut, and we take taxis around the city."

"Taxis are a luxury," Randy points out.

I shift uncomfortably in my chair. "Do you play cards?" I pull a deck out of my bag and offer it to him. Cards and board games are allowed in the dining room. Randy calls a friend over and the four of us settle into a game of bid whist.

Over the next few days, Candy and I meet up with Randy to go swimming and hiking. I find out that he doesn't belong to Jack and Jill, so there is no chance of seeing him at a dance. No need for him to join, really. He lives in a predominantly Black neighborhood and goes to a mostly Black high school. I can tell he's liked a girl before. He even mentions that he has dated a few girls in his school.

"Dated," I repeat.

"You know, go out to the movies. Grab a piece of pizza. Don't kids do that in Connecticut?"

I laugh. "Probably, but I'm just in junior high. We don't date yet."

I can tell that Candy is getting a little tired of the two of us. But I'm going to miss hanging out with Randy. I wish camp lasted one more week. It would give me time to get to know him better.

* * *

It's a free day. Campers are encouraged to enjoy activities of their choosing. Candy and I talk Randy into rowboating.

"I don't really swim well," he reminds us.

"We'll all wear life preservers. If the boat tips over, I'll pull you to shore," I say. "But don't worry, it's hard to tip a rowboat. Come on. It's fun."

He reluctantly follows us, stepping one foot tentatively into the boat. Then the other foot. Once he's inside, Candy and I take the oars and start rowing. I watch Randy closely, chatting as I paddle along, hoping to make him more comfortable. Randy grips the sides of the boat. It rocks a bit. I can imagine that being out in the middle of deep water and not knowing how you'd save yourself could be scary to a non-swimmer. I'm proud of Randy for not making us take him back to shore. "You did good," I tell him as soon as we're back.

"Next time, I choose the activity," he says, smiling and cheerful now that he's on land.

There's not much more time for another activity; it's our last night at camp. We head in different directions to change for dinner. We promise to save Randy and his friend John a seat in the dining hall. I wear a blue sundress and sandals, hoping to look good and impress Randy. I'm nervous about saying goodbye. What if he tries to kiss me? So far, we haven't ever been alone. I've never been kissed by a boy. The thought is scary and exciting at the same time. I'm certain Randy's an expert at kissing. He has to be. Right?

After dinner, the counselors hand out camp prizes. Candy gets a prize for high jump. I win one for distance swimming. Randy gets two awards, for basketball and archery. He slides beside me as the ceremony comes to a close.

"I hate to say goodbye," he whispers.

"Me, too," I admit.

"Will you call me?"

"Maybe," I reply, because calling from Stamford to the Bronx is a toll call. Mom and Dad would see the number on their phone bill and ask me about it. I need their permission to make a long-distance call. It makes me wonder if I have to get my parents' permission to like a boy. *Will I ever see Randy again?* My mind is going crazy. *Do I care if I never see him again? Maybe we'll see each other again next year at the Chock full o'Nuts camp. Will there be another one?*

"Just in case, I will give you my number," Randy offers. "Meet me outside the dining hall in ten minutes. Okay?"

I hesitate before agreeing. *Should I tell Candy?*

I whisper to Candy that I'm meeting Randy and will be back to the dorm a few minutes late. She shoots me a warning.

"It's no big deal. He's giving me his number. That's all."

"If you're not back in the dorm in twenty minutes, I'll come looking for you," she tells me.

"All right," I say.

I spot Randy standing beside the front steps. Campers race down them laughing and cheering the end of camp. I walk up to Randy with shaky knees. *Is this it?*

"I like you, Sharon Robinson," he says quietly.

I'm speechless.

"Here's my number. Please call me," he says, handing me a folded-up white paper.

Then Randy leans in. It's so quick I have no time to think about the right moves. Our lips touch. Then to my surprise, he pushes his tongue between my lips and I jerk away. Yuck!

I can't even speak. I run away so fast that I almost beat Candy back to the dorm. My cheeks are hot. I'm breathing fast. I'm holding back tears.

"What happened?" Candy asks.

"He stuck his tongue in my mouth. It was disgusting!"

Candy cracks up.

"It's not funny," I tell her.

"It's called a French kiss."

"What? How do you know about it? This isn't France."

Candy laughs some more. "I read about French kissing. And obviously you don't have to be in France."

"I never want to kiss a boy again," I protest, a bit too much. I look over at Candy and we start to giggle, then fall on our cots laughing our heads off.

"Well, at least you got kissed," she says when we've gotten the giggles out of the way.

"Yeah...next time I'll tell the boy up front: No tongues allowed."

CHAPTER 25

When I first get home from camp, I'm still trying to sort out everything that happened. My mood shifts between remembering how much fun I had and how things ended with Randy, even though he apologized. The next day, I'm in my room when there's a knock on the door.

"Can I come in?"

I'm sitting on the floor, listening to music. "Hey, Jackie."

He walks in and drops to the floor beside me.

"So, what's up?"

"Nothing."

"Doesn't seem like nothing. You came home from camp all happy one day, and the next you've got nothing to say. Doesn't add up. Did something happen?"

"Maybe."

"What happened?"

"I met a boy," I say, looking away.

"And . . ."

"Don't worry. I'll never see him again."

"Because?"

"He lives somewhere in the Bronx. Doesn't belong to Jack and Jill, so we won't be meeting up at some dance. Besides, I never want to see Randy again. He stuck his tongue in my mouth," I report, letting the words purposely run together. I hadn't given much thought to how disappointed I was in the first kiss. Now it's out like a fresh pimple.

"Not a crime . . . but the wrong kiss for a young girl like you."

"Kiss?" I object. "True, our lips touched . . . which was cool, but then he stuck his tongue in my mouth . . . and . . . it was so creepy."

Jackie chuckles. "You shouldn't have been alone with a boy anyway. You're too young, Sharon. But tell me. How did you react?"

"I shoved him hard and ran back to the girls' dorm."

"Good girl," Jackie says, slapping me on the back. "That's exactly what you should have done. You put Randy in his place and showed him you have standards. Bet he regrets that move."

"He apologized the next day," I say.

"Look, sis . . . seems like you handled things. Boys try to push girls. Glad you stopped him, but why the sad face?"

"Not sure," I admit. "I'm not the only one who walks around with a sad face," I add, hoping my brother doesn't get mad that I'm hinting about him at home. "Now that I've met and been around Black kids, it makes me kind of sad to come back to Cascade Road and live far from any of my Black friends."

"At least you have Candy," Jackie says.

"That's true," I reply, then study my brother more closely. "Must be hard for you to live so far away from your town friends, right?"

"It is, but I'm old enough to get around," Jackie reminds me. "Soon, I'll have my driver's license."

"You really live in the pool hall, you know."

"They only judge you by how many games you rack up. I'm really good at pool, so guys look up to me. Plus, I make some money. But back to your question . . . this country living is perfect for little kids. Harder for teens. There's not much to do," Jackie says.

"I used to be so happy here," I tell him. "Now I feel like I belong somewhere else. Going off to camp with other Black kids made me realize what I was missing. Coming home reminds me of how little I fit in. Do you know what I mean?"

"Look, Sharon, don't worry so much about fitting in. You are different in so many great ways. Enjoy it. You're kind, funny, and fun to be around. Don't let anyone make you feel like there's something wrong with you. You got guts, girl. I don't know any other girls like you," Jackie says.

I am stunned. I had no idea that my big brother even noticed me anymore. He always seems so disconnected to us and wrapped up in his own world. "Gee, Jackie . . . you never said any of this to me before."

"I'm saying it now, Sharon. You're the happy one. I hate seeing you down. It's not easy being a Robinson. It comes with such high expectations and not enough praise. But Mom and Dad are really proud of you. I wish I had more figured out at your age," Jackie says.

"If you had, what would you have done differently?"

"Good question." Jackie takes a moment to think. "Made some different moves, that's for sure. School and I don't get along . . . but I'm good with my hands. I don't know. It's so hard not having a name of my own. This one sure gets me into trouble."

"Guess I've got nothing to complain about."

"Being a teenager ain't easy," he tells me. "Dad tells me the key is to survive. It's just beginning for you, Shar. A first kiss. Doubting yourself. Be careful. Focus on your strengths. You've got plenty."

"You know, Jackie. I'm beginning to feel that way, too."

CHAPTER 26

At the beginning of August, we find out that the entire family is going to Washington, DC, to take part in a march together. We're at the dinner table gobbling down Grandma's tamale pie. I'm about to head for seconds when Dad clears his throat.

"I have news," he says.

I don't dare move. Instead, I lean forward so I won't miss a single detail.

"I've been invited to attend a march in Washington, DC." He looks at Mom. "We've spoken about it and agree that the whole family should be there."

After the initial excitement, David, Jackie, and I fire questions at Dad.

"Will the police use fire hoses to stop us?"

"Are we going to jail?"

"Is Dr. King going to be there?"

My head is so filled with questions, I don't know what to ask next. Will we stay in a hotel? What will I wear? Will Grandma be coming with us?

"This is not Birmingham," Dad says, hoping to calm our sudden burst of anxiety. "There will be no fire hoses or dogs, and hopefully no arrests. This is supposed to be a peaceful march, and I expect everyone, including the police, will be on their best behavior. The White House is just a few blocks away."

I glance from Mom to Jackie and David and squirm in my seat. "Is it a children's march?"

"No, Sharon. Not just children," Dad says, reaching over to touch my hand. I feel my restless heart settle down. "This is a march for everyone. There will be Black and White families from across the country coming to Washington, DC, to demand jobs and freedom. I bet there will be plenty of children, too. We'll march through the street, sing songs, link arms, hold signs, and listen to speeches. It's going to be a long, hot, crowded, and very exciting day. If we reach anywhere near the anticipated numbers, it will also be an historic day."

"Are we marching to the White House?"

"No, we'll march the National Mall from the Washington Monument to the foot of the Lincoln Memorial," Mom explains.

"Is that like from our front door to the end of our driveway?" David asks.

"It's more like from our house to High Ridge Road," Mom says.

"That's more than a mile!" I cry out.

Dad chuckles. "And you walk it all the time," he reminds us. "The actual distance between the Washington Monument and the Lincoln Memorial is just under two miles. Once we reach that point, there'll be a stage. The march will end and the speeches will begin."

"Will there be chairs for all those people?" I ask, trying to visualize the day. No one has gotten up from the table to remove their plate, go to the bathroom, or get another drink. My throat is dry.

"Most of the crowd will stand or sit on the ground," Dad says.

On the ground, I think. How will they see the speakers? What about food and water? A bathroom?

"Are you speaking?" Jackie asks Dad.

"It's come up, but most of the speakers are leaders of organizations, so I doubt if they'll ask me to speak. Most people are coming to hear Dr. King," Dad says, excusing himself and walking into the kitchen for more iced tea. I follow him.

"Dad, will we bring a picnic lunch?"

He rubs my head. "We're working on that," he tells me. "Are you afraid?"

I pour myself a glass of milk. "Maybe a little...mostly excited!" I follow Dad back into the dining room with my glass in hand. I set it on the table and slide into my chair.

"How come the march stops at the Lincoln Memorial?" David asks.

"It's fitting; it's a very grand monument. The statue of Lincoln is one hundred feet high. It's a symbol of freedom. We'll go there before the march so you can see the statue up close," Mom says.

"There's a picture of it in my history book," I tell them.

"Are we going to drive to DC?" Jackie asks.

"We'll either take the train or one of the charter buses," Dad replies.

"Will we draw our own signs?" I ask, thinking about what words I'll write on mine.

"The march is in two weeks," Dad says, lifting his arms to break up the questions. "We have time to figure out all the details. For now, it's best to think of this as Americans coming together to lift our collective voices to demand freedom from segregation, more jobs, and equality for all people. We want President Kennedy and Congress to feel the pressure to pass the civil rights bill. Remember we talked about family mission and legacy?"

We all nod our heads.

"Well, speaking up against injustice is part of that legacy. I'm excited that we'll do it as a family. Aren't you?"

"Very. You've always told us that we should build on our strengths and learn from our failures," I say. "I guess the same is true for the movement. They had success in Birmingham and are now taking their demands directly to the president of the United States. That's progress!"

Dad chuckles. "This is what I love about you kids . . . you don't see just black and white. You look deeper into people and find relationships. Rae and I couldn't be more proud of each of you," Dad says, wiping his right eye. "You truly care about other people. You also question things that seem unfair. Your mother and I know that it hasn't been easy for you to find your place here in Connecticut. But you haven't given up. You keep struggling . . . winning some battles and losing a few, too. Life is filled with challenges. It's not a fair playing field. Your mother and I will always be there for you no matter what."

I smile over at Dad, wishing I could say something that will make him know we're okay. But Jackie isn't all right. He's struggling with school, his teachers, Dad, and himself. Dad really wants us to know that he and Mom will be there no matter what happens. I hope Jackie knows that. For now, the news of the march has us all excited and hopeful. Even my older brother.

* * *

Over the next week, plans for the march are solidified. There is an official name and a firm schedule. The March on Washington for Jobs and Freedom is to be held on Wednesday, August 28.

I can't believe this is happening! We're going to be in the middle of the action, not just sitting at the dinner table hearing about it from Dad or seeing clips on the news. I wish Candy could come, but Mom has told us, no friends. This trip is about family. Our cousin Chuckie is going to meet us in Washington, DC.

Sunday night, Mom helps me pick out several outfits for the trip. We're going down a day early so we can sightsee. When she leaves the room to check on the boys, I fold the clothes and layer them neatly into my bag. I'm excited and jumpy about the trip like it's the night before the first day in a new school. There are lots of unknowns. Will there be any violence like we've seen on television? How many people will show up? Will the police carry guns and threaten us with dogs trained to attack? "Think of it as a field trip," Mom suggested. She gave my brothers and me cards with the name and address of the Willard Hotel written on them. "This is where we're staying, in case we get separated," Mom told us.

I hum the melody from "We Shall Overcome," one of the songs from the movement, as I pack. We've been learning the words to freedom songs. My favorite is "Ain't Gonna Let Nobody Turn Me Around." I start singing it while I march around my room. I keep repeating the first verse until I'm exhausted and laughing at my own silliness. I fall dramatically to the floor and lie sprawled out on my rug until Mom comes back in.

"I can't wait to get to Washington, DC," I tell her from my position on the floor.

Mom pulls me up so we can chat and finish packing. The next day, we take a train from New York's Penn Station to Washington, DC. We reach the Willard Hotel and head straight to our adjoining rooms so we can get a good night's sleep. The march is on Wednesday, which gives us Tuesday for sightseeing.

Mom walks us over to tour the White House the next day. It's a short walk from the hotel. On the way over, she explains that the first lady, Jacqueline Kennedy, redecorated the White House and opened it up to tourists. It's ten o'clock in the morning and my hands are sweating inside the white gloves that Mom insists I wear. That mistake is nothing compared to the pain radiating through my toes in these lacy white socks and stiff new black patent-leather shoes. My pale blue cotton dress is tugging at my neck. But I don't complain. Instead, I mimic Mom's graceful stride as we wind through the Red and Blue rooms, examining china and antique furniture and hearing references to former presidents who we'd studied in American history class. Halfway through the tour, the gloves come off and are balled up and stashed in my pocketbook, and all I'm thinking about is lunch and a serious change of clothes for the afternoon.

"How was the White House tour?" Dad asks over lunch.

"All right," I say after I've ordered a cheeseburger and fries. "They need some new furniture."

"It took too long," David adds.

"I kept hoping that President Kennedy would pass by," Jackie says. "I've never seen a president up close."

"That would have been special," Dad says in agreement. "What's on the agenda for the afternoon?"

"Thought I'd take the kids to the Lincoln Memorial. They need to see it before the steps are covered with people, signs, and television cameras."

"Good idea," Dad says.

"Aww, can't we go swimming?" David asks. "It's so hot down here."

"Yeah, Mom . . . can't we?" I chime in.

"Maybe later," Mom offers. "What are your plans, Jack?"

"Bayard Rustin has called a meeting," Dad replies.

"Who's Bayard Rustin?" Jackie asks.

I'm surprised at how interested he's become with the march and Martin Luther King Jr. It's a good sign that Dad is finally doing something that got Jackie's attention. I hope it's the beginning of a better relationship between the two of them.

"Bayard Rustin's been a fighter for equality since the forties. He and Dr. King founded the SCLC together, and Bayard is the main organizer for the March on Washington. Dr. King gave him two months to rally organizers from across the country and he did it. It's quite a feat," Dad explains.

"Jack, does this mean you're speaking at the march?" Mom asks.

"Looks like I'll speak briefly to get the march started," Dad tells us.

I'm impressed. *Dad must really be important*, I think.

"Jackie, are you going to the Lincoln Memorial with Mom?"

Jackie shakes his head. "Nope. I need a nap."

I look over and see my parents exchange a glance, which tells me they're not happy, but they don't cause a scene. Instead, Dad stands up, leans over to kiss Mom, and heads off to his meeting. I hope Jackie won't back out of the march altogether.

By the time we step out of the hotel, I notice buses with license plates from all over the country. We continue to walk along Pennsylvania Avenue. Mom's quiet. I suppose she's worried that Jackie will get into some kind of trouble while we're sightseeing. David and I make a game out of reading license plates and keeping track of all the states. We count fifteen different states before we reach the National Mall. I'm surprised to find that the mall is not a shopping center. It's really a park with a long pool lined with museums and government buildings. David challenges me to a race from Pennsylvania Avenue to the Reflecting Pool. He beats me by a couple of seconds. Before Mom reaches us, we've taken off our sneakers and are dipping bare feet in water. David's about to wade in when Mom grabs his shirttail and pulls.

"Shucks," David says as I laugh hysterically.

At the Lincoln Memorial, we're dwarfed by its size. I stand back, looking up in awe at the size of this huge and powerful statue. It takes a minute to regain my own strength.

"Climb up the steps," Mom urges.

I glance over at David. He nods and we take off running despite Mom's calls for us to slow down. I beat him by two seconds. We stand at Lincoln's shoes, bending over with laughter and pain in the middle of our bodies.

"Turn around and look back," Mom says, sitting beside us on one of the steps. The statue of Abraham Lincoln is at our backs and we're peering across to the Reflecting Pool. It's long and narrow with grass on either side of it. From a distance, the pool now appears to be smaller than when we were up close to it.

Mom begins to tell us about A. Philip Randolph and his organization, the Brotherhood of Sleeping Car Porters. He'd organized a mass march in Washington, DC, in the forties and fifties and joined with the SCLC to organize this march. Bayard Rustin, the man Dad went to meet with, also worked with A. Philip Randolph.

"Picture a mass of people that stretches from here to the end of the pool." Mom points far into the distance. "That's what it will be like tomorrow. There will be people as far as your eyes can see. That's the message we'll be sending out into the world. It's time to pass the Civil Rights Act and give Negroes equal rights to housing, jobs, and voting."

I look where she is pointing, trying to imagine all the people. Trying to imagine that future.

CHAPTER 27

I wake up before the sun rises. It's Wednesday and almost time to march! I put on my favorite light blue cotton dress with short sleeves. The boys are in button-down cotton shirts. David's is blue. Jackie's is white. We all wear sneakers. Mom brushes my shoulder-length dark brown hair and pulls it back into a ponytail so tight that my scalp screams back in protest. I lift my fingers toward the point of agony and Mom eases the tight clamp on my hair before we head down to the lobby.

The Willard Hotel is alive with eager march organizers and speakers.

We step outside the hotel and are greeted by a mass of people so deep I feel dizzy stepping off the sidewalk. We've been warned to be on our best behavior. Looking around, I can see that the signs carried by those assembling for the march reflect the demands for passage of the Civil Rights Act, the end of segregation, and equal job opportunities for Negroes.

Mom prepared us for the presence of armed soldiers, but seeing them with huge guns reminds me of war and the scenes from Birmingham. Feeling insecure, I grab my mother's hand. She squeezes it and smiles down at me. "We will be fine."

"Mr. Robinson," a voice calls from behind us. "My name is Michael. We met briefly last night. I've been sent to escort you and your family to the holding area."

"I remember," Dad says, shaking the young man's hand.

"Good to see you." Dad makes the introductions. "Michael is a student at Howard University here in Washington, DC. It is one of our fine Black colleges," Dad tells us. "Dr. King and I received honorary doctorates from there in 1957."

"I didn't know that," Michael says. "That is so cool."

"Michael, where are you taking us?" Mom asks.

"There is a reserved area for dignitaries. Your husband will be speaking to the crowd before the start of the march. We'll head there now. We're early, so expect to be there an hour or more before he speaks," he explains.

"Okay. We'll follow you," Dad says.

Our walk is slowed by the sheer volume of people on the sidewalks and in the middle of Constitution Avenue. I can hardly see the pavement. Folks of all ages and colors mill around and shout out to Mom and Dad as we pass. Laughter and song fill the air. It is already steamy. Between the crowds and security forces, I feel anxious. I use the handkerchief in my dress pocket to wipe away sweat.

We pass water stations and signs telling us to stay hydrated. I yank on Mom's arm and she asks Michael to stop so we can drink water. Along the way, I read more signs calling for equality, racial justice, and the end of Jim Crow. I also see signs calling for unity and freedom. As soon as we reach the mall, we are welcomed into the holding area. Television cameras and giant speakers are placed near a platform. Michael points to the platform in the distance and tells us that Dad will stand beside Dr. Martin Luther King Jr. and speak from there.

Wow! I think. *That's amazing!* I watch Dad, wondering if he's nervous to speak in front of the tens of thousands of marchers, but he is smiling broadly, busy greeting people and doing radio interviews. All around us, everyone is slapping one another's backs and making introductions. Do they really expect that Dad will remember their names?

Roy Wilkins, the NAACP president, stops by along with actors Ossie Davis and Ruby Dee. Ruby Dee played my mother in the 1950 Jackie Robinson movie, and she tells me a story about the time that she held me during a break from filming when I was one month old and Mom brought me to visit the set. I loved hearing that from Ruby. It adds a hint of intimacy to the march as more people crowd into the roped-off space.

I wiggle about, impatient for the march to begin, when a voice comes over the loudspeaker giving directions and encouraging people to form lines. From where we stand, I can't see a beginning or an end. I've never been in such a crowd before. That's when they came for Dad.

Several men whisk Dad and David away from Mom, Jackie, and me, promising we'll be reunited when the marching stops. Michael stays with us. I feel sweat seep down my neck and roll down my back. My palms are sweaty as well. Mom grabs my hand.

We're at a standstill. Voices come over the loudspeaker welcoming us. I yank Mom's arm at the sound of Dad's voice. It's loud and clear. I lift up onto my toes, trying to see my father through the bodies surrounding me. It's impossible. Michael leans down to tell me that Dad and Dr. King are standing on the steps of the Lincoln Memorial. I grin up at Michael, excited by the news. "That's so cool," I say as Dad welcomes the marchers and tells them that he's traveled with his wife and three children to be a part of this great day.

"I know all of us are going to go away feeling we cannot turn back," Dad says, and the crowd roars in response.

Just knowing that he's standing next to Martin Luther King Jr. thrills me. I remember Dad telling me about another time they were together. It was last year at the SCLC's annual dinner in Birmingham, Alabama. Afterward, Dad showed me his speech, pointing out a section where he talked about his dream for my brothers and me.

"All I want for my children . . . and I think all you want for yours . . . is a fair and equal chance and respect for their dignity as human beings. Give us that and we'll do the rest."

We'd talked about this statement on the trip to Washington. Dad explained to me that we often first see the future in a dreamlike state. Our goals and plans seem lofty. But when given equal access to good education, determination, and a willingness to struggle, we can make our dreams come true.

A thundering voice tells us it's time to start the march! The crowd roars back in response and line after line of people surge forward. It's not fast-paced like I'd imagined it would be. The sheer volume of people makes that impossible, but we're singing freedom songs and shouting out slogans in a call and response so it seems to me that we're sprinting along. I am so excited to be a part of the moment that I forget about the heat and the need to stay hydrated.

Mom, Jackie, Michael, and I are in a line close to the front. I know this because Michael keeps us oriented. We can't see a true beginning or end, but we can see President Abraham Lincoln. He towers over us from a distance. I am happy that Mom took us to visit yesterday. It gives me some perspective. Some of my neighbors have linked arms. I hold tight to Mom's hand and join the others in the singing of the day's anthem:

"We are not afraid. We are not afraid."

As we finish singing the first verse of "We Shall Overcome," the wave of people in front of us lunges forward. Our line follows in a stop-and-start pattern. It reminds me of jumping waves in the Atlantic Ocean. In between the rush of water that can submerge and crush you, there's a break that allows you to recover and get prepared for the next wave. I stay in the moment, waiting for the next big surge toward the Lincoln Memorial.

I'm no longer dreaming of marching for freedom in Birmingham. I'm here marching alongside people from California, Alabama, Mississippi, New York, and places in between. It strikes me that we're demanding equality for Negroes, yet unlike the marches I've seen on television from Birmingham, these marchers are Black and White. It makes me feel like we're in this fight together. We've joined forces against those who hate. We're showing the world that the struggle for full equality affects all of us.

As I look around, I smile, feeling happy like I do when Diamond and I are in perfect harmony. I turn and see Black and White people stopping to hug their neighbors. "This is amazing!" a man yells out to no one in particular. "Freedom now!"

I don't wear a watch, so it's hard to tell how long we've been standing, walking, stopping, singing. But I'm aware of thirst, tired legs, and a need for food. It makes me feel anxious. Will we ever make it to the Lincoln Memorial? Will this wave of people topple over me if I fall? I look up at Mom, but she doesn't see me. Her face is forward. I can't see Jackie's face either. What if we get separated?

My head begins to spin. Knees feel like they'll give out. Then everything goes blank.

* * *

I feel myself falling. Then being lifted and pulled away from the crowd. I'm aware of voices and song, but for a split second, I cannot see.

* * *

"You fainted." Mom's face and voice come in and I'm relieved. "We're in the medical tent alongside the march," Mom explains. "Michael and Jackie are with us. Dad and David are still marching at the front of the line."

"I want to march, too," I whisper.

"You've been marching," Mom reminds me. "Here, sip this water."

I lift my head off the pillow and take a few sips. "It tastes funny," I tell her.

"It's good for you. There's sugar and electrolytes in it to make you feel better quickly."

I sit up on the cot and take the plastic cup and a package of peanut butter crackers from my mother. I can see clearly again. Looking around, the place is like the nurse's office at school. There are several cots with men and women lying or sitting up, a doctor in a white coat, and a couple of others who I assume are nurses.

"Did they faint, too?" I ask Mom, snacking again on the crackers.

"Maybe," she replies, and passes me more crackers filled with peanut butter.

"My head and stomach still ache," I reply as I start on the second package of crackers.

"That feeling will go away soon as your body's had enough fluid," Mom assures me.

A man in a white coat walks over to us. "Well, young lady, are you feeling better?"

"Better," I mumble through a mouthful of peanut butter. "What happened?"

"You fainted," he replies.

"Yeah, but why?"

"It's very hot, crowded, and probably a bit scary, right?"

I nod toward him.

"A perfect setup for dehydration. Glad to see you're eating and drinking. Let us know when you feel up to walking around," the doctor tells me.

"I'm ready to go back to the march," I declare.

"Then eat up and finish your drink. We'll check you again in ten minutes. You should be ready to go then."

"Thank you," Mom says to the physician.

He has a nice smile. "My pleasure, Mrs. Robinson."

"How will we ever find Dad?" I ask Mom as soon as the doctor walks away.

"Don't worry. Michael's here. He says that we're close to where your father and David are," Mom assures me.

I swing my legs over the side of the cot, stand up, and stretch. Once I'm cleared to go, Michael leads us to the reserve section where Dad and David are waiting. The front of the line has reached the foot of the Lincoln Memorial. Dad gives me a big hug and tells me that I walked over a mile. Satisfied that I didn't miss the march altogether, I settle down as the speakers begin to walk to the stage.

A. Philip Randolph opens with a reminder to the marchers that they're part of a mass movement to combat unemployment and poverty, and to strike down segregation in its many forms. When he uses the term "revolution," it reminds me again that this struggle is like a war. The crowd cheers loudly. He is followed by other speakers, including a young man named John Lewis from the Student Nonviolent Coordinating Committee who challenges us to come south and march. After that is James

Farmer representing the Congress of Racial Equality, Whitney Young Jr. from the National Urban League, and Roy Wilkins of the National Association for the Advancement of Colored People.

The speakers are all men, which makes me wonder where all the women leaders are. The themes sound familiar. I look over at Dad, and he winks back. I try to stay focused, but I'm fighting with a desire to get up and walk around. I look over at David. He's rubbing quarters together. Jackie's been making runs to get us food and drink. I see now that he's checking out the people on the other side of the ropes.

Along the grassy areas, people look like they're having a picnic, sharing food and chatting with those around them. It looks friendly and peaceful. The crowd keeps up a steady applause when speakers hit a note they agree with. You can hear shouts of "Freedom!" and "Down with Jim Crow!" The sun has crossed over and is no longer beating directly over our heads. It feels cooler. I hear someone shout, "Bring out Dr. King!" I turn around and realize the shout came from far behind us. Now the crowd is cheering. I wonder if it was for the person who yelled for Martin Luther King or if they were applauding the current speaker.

Getting antsy, I check Mom's wristwatch. It's after four. She looks down at me and smiles. "Dr. King will speak soon," she tells me.

Someone steps up to the podium and announces that there are over two hundred thousand people in attendance. The crowd goes wild. My brothers and I join in cheering. The numbers would be hard for us to imagine if we weren't here to see.

Then something magical happens. Gospel singer Mahalia Jackson is introduced and she steps elegantly to the podium. She reminds me of an African queen with her tall proud stance and jeweled hat. A dozen microphones block my view, but the first notes silence the crowd and remind me of music I've heard at home. "How I Got Over," which she sings with power and joy, is met by synchronized clapping from the front of the line to the back. We jump up from our seats and join in clapping and humming to the beat. And the crowd parties! It feels like a celebration!

With the second song, Mahalia Jackson reminds us what's at stake if things don't change. She begins slow. It sounds almost like a woman moaning in pain. *"I've been 'buked and I've been scorned,"* she sings.

I don't understand all the words, but the message is clear. She's talking to the millions of Negroes who've come through the horrors of slavery, fought back against the violence of lynching, church bombings, and Jim Crow segregation and now stand together with White Americans demanding a change. I feel like crying as Mahalia Jackson eases away from the microphone and Dr. Martin Luther King Jr. steps up to the podium. The crowd roars!

Dr. King starts with prepared remarks: "I am happy to join with you today in what will go down in history as the greatest demonstration for freedom in the history of our nation . . ."

The applause is deafening.

Martin Luther King goes on to remind the masses of the passage of the Emancipation Proclamation and the fact that one hundred years later, Negroes are still not free. Dr. King talks about the urgency and the avoidance of bitterness and hatred. Somewhere along the way, Mahalia Jackson shouts out, "Tell them about the dream, Martin!"

Dr. King puts down his prepared remarks and looks deep into the crowd as if we're in his living room. "I say to you today, my friends, so even though we face the difficulties of today and tomorrow, I still have a dream."

The promised four-minute speech goes on for sixteen minutes as Dr. King excites all gathered. We're part of that dream. Dr. King has put aside complex sentences and speaks from his heart. His vision for America is exactly why we've all come to Washington, DC. I, too, want to live in an America where I'm judged by what I do and not how I look. It reminds me of my early days at Hoyt Elementary School, when students thought the brown color of my skin was dirt. His words tell me I am right to speak up for myself. That I have the right to be myself. That is my hope and path to freedom.

"Free at last! Free at last! Thank God Almighty, we are free at last!"

CHAPTER 28

As I head down to the stables, I wonder if Diamond will recognize me. Surely, he'll know something has changed. I feel different. More content with who I am and feeling especially good about having an actual role to play in this period of social change. Hearing Martin Luther King's speech changed me. Surely, Diamond will notice this new strength. Maybe it will come through in the way I ride him or how I hold the reins.

When I reach Diamond, I caress his face. "Diamond, I missed you," I croon. "I know David and I have been away a lot this summer, but you have to understand things have changed. We've been in Washington, DC. No, we didn't go to meet with the president, but we did tour the White House. We went to the March on Washington. There were thousands and thousands of people there from all over the United States. I know it's hard to picture what that looks like. It reminds me of being at the beach, standing on the sand and looking across the ocean, expecting to see land on the other side. Instead, you do not see the end. The sea seems to go on forever. Well, Diamond, that's how it felt looking back through a sea of people. It was endless."

Diamond snorts.

"I know . . . I wish you'd been there, too. It's no place for a horse unless we turn you into a police horse," I say, then chuckle. "Don't worry, that's not happening. You're part of our family now."

I take out his brushes and use long strokes to get out the knots and patches of dirt. I sing "This Little Light of Mine" and hum to the rhythm of "I've Been 'Buked." When Mahalia Jackson sang those words at the march, I didn't exactly know what they meant. Dad explained later that it means to be rebuked, to be criticized and disrespected. He said that Black people have relied on their faith to get beyond hardships and that Mahalia prays when she sings. That's our hope.

When Diamond is groomed and fed, we ride off our property, turning right up Cascade Road to the place where the water cascades down the rocky cliff. It is my favorite place. Today, I'm determined to let Diamond taste the fresh chilled water from the brook.

We take our time meandering along the road's curves. At the right spot, I jump off and lead Diamond into the woods on a well-beaten path. We duck under low-lying tree branches and around the rocky terrain until we reach the running water that pools at the bottom of the cliff. While Diamond enjoys his drink, I climb up onto a rock above him.

"This has been the most unbelievable summer," I say out loud as I mention the highlights: "Our first jazz concert in June, a first kiss . . . well, that didn't go so well . . . the March on Washington . . . and now Martin Luther King Jr. is coming to our house!"

Diamond lifts his head from the water and looks back at me as if he's as shocked as I am.

"That's right, Diamond! Can you believe it? We're having another jazz concert. I guess they're part of our life now, Diamond. You'll have to get used to all the people who will stop by the stables to meet you. But we don't have to think about that now. Today is a normal day. Let's be lazy."

CHAPTER 29

On September 8, we spring into action for our second Afternoon of Jazz. Mom wakes us at six in the morning with the music of Mahalia Jackson. As soon as I hear "Take My Hand, Precious Lord" blasting through the living room speakers, I jump out of bed, knocking my copy of *The Learning Tree* off my nightstand. When Mom saw I was reading it, she told me that the author, Gordon Parks, is one of her favorite photographers and that she'd keep an eye out for an exhibit of his work so we could go together. I credit my mom for our love of music, art, and books. And today's concert is going to be another chance to hear some amazing songs!

Candy, Jackie's friend Bradley Gordon, and David's friend Michael, along with our cousins, Jojo, Kirkie, and Chuckie, all stayed overnight. Within ten minutes, nine sleepy barefooted kids file out of the bedrooms to watch the sunrise. We line up outside on the porch overlooking the grounds. The stage is completely covered by a tent. The rest of the lawn is uncovered. The concert will go on, rain or shine. We have no doubt that Mom will deliver a sunny day and us kids are there to witness her powers. David starts the chant, "Come on, sun!" The nine of us repeat the chant over and over while Mom looks up to the sky and prays for sunshine. As a red-and-orange glow reaches the tops of the trees, we chant until the sun has fully risen in the sky.

Then it's all business. Mom reminds us that in four hours, fifteen hundred guests will arrive! I know that means get busy. Boy, do we scramble.

This concert will double our first one. Since the March on Washington, Dr. Martin Luther King's popularity has spiked and many of our anticipated guests say they're coming just to hear him speak.

With a sunny morning guaranteed, we scatter back to our rooms to dress and clean up. I hang up all the clothes off my closet floor, then tackle the bathroom knowing Mom will be by soon to inspect. It's a race that has my heart pumping fast.

Grandma has scrambled eggs and bacon waiting for us. We gobble breakfast and rush off to set up our soda, water, and hot dog stands. The older boys head to the front gate with Dad to go over the parking arrangements. This time, there are two off-site parking areas that need to be managed. At the same time,

Mrs. Dickerson and her welcoming committee set the table at the entrance to the property. They'll greet the guests, take tickets that have been purchased, and sell more if needed.

In the backyard, a dozen things are happening at once. The sound system is being wired and tested. We jump in fright as the first music blasts through the giant speakers to the right of the soda and hot dog stands. "Sorry!" the sound technicians shout as they work to get the music at the right level.

Up from our stand, a small tent is being erected. It's the medical tent. It brings a flashback of the one I woke up in at the march. An emergency vehicle will be on hand as well.

By eight, volunteers swarm the grounds, getting ready for the guests, who will start arriving when the gates open at ten. The concert starts at noon. We wave to our guests, who are burdened with armfuls of blankets and baskets of food. It's going to be some picnic. I am so happy seeing it all come together and knowing it will be one of the most exciting days of our lives!

No one knows what to expect from Dr. King. We prepare our parents' bedroom with its private screened-in porch for him just in case, although the hope is that he'll spend most of the time outdoors interacting with the guests.

Proceeds from this concert will go to the Southern Christian Leadership Conference and the National Association for the Advancement of Colored People, the two national civil rights organizations that Dad has supported for years. Last night, he gave us kids a quick history lesson. We didn't have to memorize all the facts, just a few in case someone asked us questions. As I open bags of hot dogs rolls and place them in the tray, I test my memory. The NAACP was founded in 1909, I repeat silently. Its lawyers work on justice and equality cases and are responsible for passage of major anti-lynching and discrimination legislation. Roy Wilkins is the president and he's expected today, too.

The Southern Christian Leadership Conference was founded in Atlanta, Georgia, but is best known for the bus boycott in Montgomery, Alabama. Dr. Martin Luther King Jr. is president. Their philosophy is to use nonviolent confrontation to break down segregation and discrimination. "Got it," I say as I take the last of the rolls out of the plastic bags.

Dad tells us that every dollar we raise is important. He leans over the young volunteers and says, "Sell hot dogs, sodas, and the good work of the organizations." As we prepare our stands, I can tell that each kid is on a personal mission to raise as much money as they can.

The concert kicks off at noon sharp! Some of the jazz musicians are famous while others are launching their careers. All the music is great! Our guests clap and cheer as the musicians come and go.

When flutist Herbie Mann arrives, I proudly announce that I'm taking flute lessons.

"Go get your flute," he tells me.

I race up the hill, through the house to my bedroom, to grab my flute, then run back down to the stage with it cradled in my arms.

"Let's go," he says to me. "I'll give you a lesson."

Mom and Dad look on while I join Herbie Mann for a quick number. It's one of the highlights of my day!

There are many more special moments, like David playing the drums with Carlos Valdes. I sit on the stage watching while jazz pianist Billy Taylor ushers more than forty-two musicians on and off the stage.

We work in two-hour shifts so everyone can take a break and meet up with their families. The big question, of course, is when will Dr. King arrive?

In the middle of the afternoon, Mom sends someone down to our stand to get David and me. We race up the hill and through the back door into the house, where Mom hurries us out the front door just as the car carrying Dr. King pulls into our circular driveway.

I stand shyly beside my mother as she steps forward to greet Dr. King while he's getting out of the car. My insides are jumping with excitement. His warm smile is the first thing I notice. It settles me down as Dad makes the introductions.

Dr. King extends his hand to me and I take it, feeling a surge of pride and warmth. "We saw you speak at the March on Washington," I say softly. "I liked when you talked about your children."

"I was so happy that you and your brothers came down to Washington. Your father is so proud of you all. When we were together in Birmingham last year, he told me that you asked to come down with him. You have your father and mother's courageous and generous spirit."

I beam up at my father, completely in love with Dr. King. I watch as he bends to greet David and draws Jackie into a hug.

"Jackie has been helping his father park cars and greet our guests while Sharon and David and their friends run the hot dog and soda stands," Mom shares with Dr. King.

"At our last jazz concert, we raised over a thousand dollars for Birmingham," I add.

"We'll make even more money this time," David tells him.

"That's wonderful," Dr. King says, looking from Jackie down to David and me. "There are a number of kids in Birmingham who were able to get out of jail because of your work. Your father has been telling me that you kids integrated your schools and neighborhood. In the movement, we refer to folks like you as 'foot soldiers.'"

I'm delighted by Dr. King's acknowledgment that we, too, play a role in the movement to end segregation.

"That's a funny name," David says, giggling.

"It means that you, like thousands of children across the country, are the unsung heroes of the civil rights movement," Dr. King tells us.

His words resonate in my heart. I repeat them softly feeling the sense of isolation drifting away. Mom sends Jackie, David, and me back to work and she and Dad usher Dr. King inside the house to make him comfortable and share him with the others.

When I get back to the soda stand, I report that Martin Luther King has arrived. We jump around, then calm down, motivated to sell sodas for double the price.

Not long after they arrive, I see Dr. King and Roy Wilkins wandering the hillside, speaking to the guests. The sight of them sparks increased competition among the kids.

"Give it up for the children in Birmingham." We push our customers to give a bit extra for the causes by adding slogans to our sales pitch. "Don't forget the brave lawyers!"

I watch Dr. King meander over to the stage to chat and laugh with the musicians, and I realize that he is comfortable with all types of people. Mom and Dad come down to the stand to get David and me. We find a clear spot on the lawn in front of the stage so we can listen as a family to Roy Wilkins and Martin Luther King.

A jazzy rendition of "We Shall Overcome" signals the shift from music to speeches. We clap along as Roy Wilkins is introduced. He thanks us all for supporting the work of the NAACP, then hands the mic to Dr. King.

I cross my legs and rest my elbows on my knees. Dr. King has my full attention. Glancing over at my parents, I see that they're leaning into each other and listening. Dr. King thanks my parents and tells the crowd that my father is "one of those great unselfish souls." It reminds me that Dad never complains about the cross-country fund-raising trips. In fact, he comes home inspired.

Dr. King continues by thanking all the volunteers and jazz fans before launching into his special message for all of us.

"We're in the midst of great social change," Dr. King informs us. "But it is hard for many to recognize."

I glance over at my parents, thankful that our family has centered their lives around this movement. Dr. King's words echo ones I'd heard at home. But then, he startles me away from the happy place of the moment into a darker one.

"Some may even have to suffer physical death to save the children from psychological death," Dr. King declares. I clap along with the crowd, but my mind is stuck on Dr. King's words. *Who is going to die?* I wonder. And what does Dr. King mean when he says, 'save the children from psychological death'? Is this a feeling of hopelessness that he's anticipating? Or is it a warning that we're at war? The same war I've been worried about since my birthday weekend, when George Wallace proclaimed his belief and desire to maintain segregation forever. I feel a chill. But the day ends with all of us feeling a sense of hope.

CHAPTER 30

Seven days later, Addie Mae Collins, Cynthia Wesley, Carole Robertson, and Denise McNair are killed when a bomb blows through stained-glass windows at the Sixteenth Street Baptist Church in Birmingham, Alabama. A church that played a major role in the Children's March.

Church bombings are not new. They're used to strike terror. But this attack is so evil. It happens just after Sunday school, before church services. And the victims are innocent girls around my age. The news breaks me down. I'm devastated and insecure. It makes me question the good feelings I'd had from the March on Washington and our wonderful jazz concerts. *Can we win this war?* I wonder.

A few days later, Dad tells us that Dr. King gave the eulogy at the funeral service for three of the girls. He also says that the title of the sermon planned before the bombing was going to be "A Love that Forgives." I hear the words but can't imagine how that is possible. The pain this crime has caused the girls' families, Birmingham, and the movement is unbearable. I've never known this deep level of hate. Where does it come from? After dinner, I head straight to my room and climb into bed. I am under the covers, still in my school clothes, when Dad knocks on my door.

I force myself to sit up as he comes into the room and sits on the edge of my bed. He puts his hand over mine without saying a word. Tears stream down my cheeks so he wraps an arm around my shoulders.

"Wish I could make this better, Shar," he whispers in a raspy voice that suggests he's cried as well.

"It's so horrible and unfair," I sob.

"This is the worst news possible. A tragedy that has left us with two choices. We can give up in defeat. Or we can use our anger and sorrow to keep fighting against hatred. I intend to fight," Dad says. "I've already sent off letters to President Kennedy and members of Congress, trying to force them to make some good out of this horror by passing the civil rights laws. The lives stolen from these innocent girls should sound moral outrage in every human being. Our leaders must send that signal out now." Dad hands me a handkerchief. "Sharon, I cannot promise you that the passage of any law will eliminate hate. But the laws will give Negroes full citizenship and bring us closer to equality."

I blow my nose and swing my legs over the edge. Dad smiles down at me. We sit side by side with our legs touching.

"I bet our Jack and Jill chapter will organize a letter-writing campaign. Our congressmen need to hear from kids like us, too," I proclaim. "And we can have another jazz concert to raise money for the girls' families, right, Dad?"

He chuckles and pats my knee. "It's already under discussion."

"Then, Dad," I say, standing up and looking in my father's eyes, "I choose action."

I follow Dad to the living room, where the rest of the family is gathered. We talk about the tragedy and shared family mission, knowing that with faith, family, justice, love, and time, we will heal and thrive. But we're also reminded that the struggle for freedom is ongoing.

Mom gets up from the couch, walks over to our record collection, finds what she's looking for, and puts on one of our favorite gospel songs: "This Little Light of Mine."

As the song starts, I look around the room at my family. And we are all together, each of us listening to the words, knowing that we cannot give up. The fight goes on.

THIS LITTLE LIGHT OF MINE

This little light of mine, I'm gonna let it shine.
This little light of mine, I'm gonna let it shine.
This little light of mine, I'm gonna let it shine.
Let it shine, let it shine, let it shine.

Everywhere I go, I'm gonna let it shine.
Everywhere I go, I'm gonna let it shine
Everywhere I go, I'm gonna let it shine.
Let it shine, let it shine, let it shine.

AUTHOR'S NOTE AND ACKNOWLEDGMENTS

At thirteen, my understanding of the world was shaken up by the brutal attack on the children marching peacefully for freedom in Birmingham, Alabama. It opened my eyes to a new level of racial injustice. There were kids my age (and younger!) taking part in the civil rights movement. At the time, I dreamed of going to Birmingham and linking arms with them. *Child of the Dream* tells my recollection of these events from 1963, from my thirteenth birthday in January to the bombing of the Sixteenth Street Baptist Church that tragically killed four young girls in September of that year. It was a year of major change for both the country and myself, and it continued on in that manner.

On November 22, 1963, John Fitzgerald Kennedy, the thirty-fifth president of the United States, was assassinated in Dallas, Texas. Like the rest of the country, I remember being shocked and scared. Later that day, Lyndon B. Johnson was sworn in as the thirty-sixth president.

Before his death, President Kennedy had proposed civil rights legislation that would end segregation in public places and ban employment discrimination on the basis of race, color, religion, sex, or national origin. But he was unable to get the bill through Congress. After his death, President Johnson was able to maneuver a version of the bill to passage, signing the Civil Rights Act of 1964 into law on July 2, 1964.

While this provided equal rights under the law, it still did not ensure those rights in practice as protests in Selma against lack of voting rights and the Chicago Freedom Movement for equal housing, employment, health, and education protections continued in 1965.

On April 4, 1968, Dr. Martin Luther King Jr. was assassinated while standing on the balcony of the Lorraine Motel in Memphis, Tennessee. I was shocked and deeply saddened by the violence against another great leader, especially one who'd dedicated his life to peace. Thankfully, Dr. King's legacy continues to grow and have an impact on the world.

Even now, we're reminded daily of how far we've come since 1963. Yet the struggle for justice and equality for all continues. My hope is that both the progress of the past and the hope for the future will continue to inspire others to lift their voices for freedom.

Fifty-five years after I first imagined linking arms with the children of the Children's March, I traveled to Birmingham at the invitation of Janice Nixon and Ann Jimerson. Many of the original march participants were convening to attend a remembrance of the Sixteenth Street Baptist Church bombing. It was a day of cherished memories and powerful emotions. The dream I held as a child to meet these incredible children involved in the civil rights movement had finally come true.

* * *

Mom, thank you for saving our letters, report cards, and photographs, as well as my diary from 1962, and for nurturing in us a love for music, books, and fine art. I cherish our friendship and enduring love.

Thank you to my family: My son, Jesse, whom I miss desperately and will carry in my heart always. My brother, David, and sister-in-law, Ruti. My nieces: Sonya, Susan, Ayo, Meta, Rachel, Raheli, Faith, Nubia, and Onia. And nephews: Saburi and Busaro. My daughter-in-law, Tatiane. And my beloved grandchildren, Lucas and Jessica.

A special thank-you to the many talented, wonderful women and men at Scholastic, most especially my extraordinary editor Matt Ringler, who is both wise and kind. Matt's enthusiasm for *Child of the Dream* was matched only by his loving attention to detail. Matt, thank you for believing in my storytelling and writing skills while not being afraid to challenge me to dig deeper.

Many, many thanks to Dick Robinson and Ellie Berger. My publicist and friend, Charisse Meloto. The publicity team and Tracy van Straaten. The marketing team and Rachel Coun. Lizette Serrano and her team. Art director, Elizabeth Parisi. Maeve Norton, Shelly Romero, Josh Berlowitz, Emily Teresa, and Tonya Leslie. A special thank-you to cover artist Britney Symone. I was blown away by your creation. Welcome to children's publishing! Also, special thanks to Christopher Paul Curtis and Andrea Davis Pinkney for the incredible words and ongoing encouragement and friendship.

Thank you to my agent, Katherine Cowles. We call her Kitty. It fits her playful, positive attitude without taking away from her brilliant advice, firm negotiating skills, and dogged determination.

I couldn't have written this book without the remembrances of several of my lifelong friends. Most especially: Candace Allen, Kimberly Allen-King, and Twanda Bowers. Our sisterhood began in Stamford, Connecticut, and has endured despite long separations and lifestyles that have taken each of us far from where we initially bonded. Thank you for revisiting our early adolescent days and for agreeing to share portions of your own stories with our readers.

I'd also like to thank my dear friends and recent acquaintances: Janus Adams (historian), for her studied research and perspective on the Birmingham Campaign. Mike Milone (research psychologist), for his invaluable feedback. The Schomburg Center for Research in Black Culture. LeRoy Simmons, from the Civil Rights Institute. Mike Mueller from Scholastic. Maureen Costello at the Southern Poverty Law Center. James and Gloria Nelson and all the men and women I met who are members of Kids in Birmingham 1963—an online community founded by Ann Jimerson. Dale Long and

Janis Nixon were two members of this community who spent hours with me reliving their experiences from Birmingham in 1963.

I'm a writer who works best with structure: A desk. A laptop. Walls plastered with timelines and story arcs. Quiet. Mimi (my five-pound Morkie) perched in her bed on my desk. But I like to edit chapters surrounded by voices. Caffe Luna Rosa, a beachside restaurant in Delray Beach, Florida, became my go-to spot. Its warm, welcoming staff; a table by the open windows; and a peek at the Atlantic Ocean got me through rewrites of chapter after chapter.

And most of all, thank you to my young readers. You are the future!

Inspiring and moving stories from
SHARON ROBINSON

Including the biographies about baseball legend and civil rights icon, Jackie Robinson!